W9-CFI-966

A Retreat With Peter

Other titles in the A Retreat With... *Series:*

A RETREAT WITH PETER

Growing From Sinner to Saint

Rev. Jim Willig
Tammy Bundy

ST. ANTHONY MESSENGER PRESS
Cincinnati, Ohio

Special thanks to our consultant, JULIE GRIPPA,
for offering her time, talent, insight and inspiration.

Scripture citations are taken from the *New Revised Standard Version Bible*, copyright ©1989 by the Division of Christian Education of the National Council of Churches of Christ in the U.S.A. and used by permission.

Lyrics from Stephen Schwartz's, "Day By Day," from the musical *Godspell*, copyright ©1971, by Range Road Music Inc., Quartet Music Inc. and New Cadenza Music Corporation, are reprinted by permission of the Hal Leonard Corporation and Carlin America, Inc.

Lyrics from Oscar Hammerstein II's, "Climb Every Mountain," from *The Sound of Music*, copyright ©1965 and "You'll Never Walk Alone," from *Carousel*, copyright ©1941, are reprinted by permission of Williamson Music.

Lyrics from Sebastian Temple's "Prayer of St. Francis," copyright ©1967, OCP Publications and dedicated to Mrs. Frances Tracy, are reprinted by permission of OCP Publications.

Lyrics from Dan Schutte's "Here I Am, Lord," copyright ©1981, Daniel L. Shutte and New Dawn Music, are reprinted by permission of OCP Publications.

Cover illustration by Steve Erspamer, S.M.
Cover and book design by Mary Alfieri

ISBN 0-86716-466-2

Copyright ©2001, Jim Willig and Tammy Bundy

All rights reserved.

Library of Congress Cataloging-in-Publication Data

Willig, Jim, 1951-
  A retreat with Peter : growing from sinner to saint / Jim Willig, Tammy M. Bundy.
      p. cm. — (A retreat with— series)
Includes bibliographical references.
  ISBN 0-86716-466-2 (pbk.)
  1. Spiritual retreats—Catholic Church. 2. Peter, the Apostle, Saint. 3. Imaginary conversations. I. Bundy, Tammy M., 1961- II. Title. III. Series.
  BX2375 .W55 2001
  269'.6—dc21

                                    2001005104

Published by St. Anthony Messenger Press
www.AmericanCatholic.org
Printed in the U.S.A.

To Saint Peter
*for leading the way
on this journey
through humanness
to holiness.*

*And to all our companions
on this journey—
it is with love,
we dedicate this book.*

FATHER JIM WILLIG COULD ALWAYS IDENTIFY WITH SAINT PETER.

He often said that the fact that the Lord could use Peter in such a great way, in spite of his human weakness, gave the rest of us hope.

And Father Jim gave us hope as well.

We wrote this book during the very last months of Father Jim's life—finishing it only three weeks before his death at the age of fifty. And as we wrote about Peter and his understandable struggle with picking up his cross and following Jesus, we became incredibly aware of how Father Jim's cross of cancer connected these two men even more. For this reason, Father Jim's voice can be heard in parts of this retreat. All of the introductory comments in the "Coming Together in the Spirit" sections are from Father Jim, as he relates to Peter and shares the struggle and ultimate joy that he found in carrying his cross of cancer.

Father Jim often believed that it was Peter's great love of the Lord that was responsible for the Lord choosing to use Peter in such a beautiful and inspiring way. I believe the same can be said of Father Jim Willig. He was more like his beloved Saint Peter than he ever knew.

And it was a privilege and a pleasure for me to work with them both.

Tammy Bundy

Contents

Introducing A Retreat With...

Several years ago, Gloria Hutchinson took up the exhortation once given to Thomas Merton: "Keep on writing books that make people love the spiritual life." Through her own writing and that of many gifted others, Gloria brought flesh and format to this retreat series.

It is with a deep appreciation for her foresight that I have assumed the role of series editor. Those of you who have returned to this series again and again will not be jarred by the changes; they are few and subtle. Those of you who are new will find, I hope, that God works to reach us in any manner we will permit, if we but take the time to come aside for a while and wait for the spirit.

The many mentors who have come to life in the pages of this series are not meant to be a conglomeration of quotes by and about them. They are intimate portraits, drawn by authors who know their subject well. But just as our viewing of the Mona Lisa tells us more about ourselves than about Leonardo's relationship with his mysterious subject, so the real value in these retreats comes from the minds and hearts of their readers. You are invited to dream and doubt, muse and murmur. If you find a mentor's words compelling, the end of each book has a list of resources to deepen your acquaintance. If you find some of your mentor's ideas challenging, or even disturbing, you can be sure the spirit is at work.

Come aside for a while...

Kathleen Carroll
Series Editor

Getting to Know Our Director

"And I tell you, you are Peter, and on this rock
I will build my church..."
                    —Matthew 16:18

Peter.

Jesus gave him a name that means "rock." The name he was given at birth, though, was Simon.

Just as he has two distinct names, he also has two distinct sides. He is gentle, but bold; foolish, yet wise; cowardly, but brave. In other words, he was human. It is Peter's baffling blend of human weaknesses and strengths that make him especially lovable to so many people. He willingly leaves life as he once knew it to start following Jesus. Yet he thinks nothing of asking in a completely childish fashion, "Look, we have left everything and followed you. What then will we have?" (Matthew 19:27).

Peter proudly professes that Jesus is the Messiah, only to have Jesus affirm that, "Blessed are you, Simon son of Jonah! For flesh and blood has not revealed this to you, but my Father in heaven" (Matthew 16:17). But before those powerfully praising words could sink in, Peter immediately becomes the reluctant recipient of Jesus' anger when Peter objects to the idea of a suffering Messiah. Peter's pride will tumble when he hears Jesus respond to him, "Get behind me, Satan! You are a stumbling block to me; for you are setting your mind not on divine things but on human things" (Matthew 16:23). It is truly amazing that one minute Peter is inspired by

God, the Father himself, to reveal the most profound truth about who Jesus is. Then, the very next minute, almost in the same breath, Peter is influenced by Satan and becomes a stumbling block to Jesus. Something about this man held great potential for both good and bad at the same time. Perhaps this is another reason why we so easily identify with Peter—perhaps we recognize those same tendencies within ourselves.

These two sides of Peter's personality establish the rich relationship he has with Jesus. He wants to put his best foot forward, but so often ends up putting his foot in his mouth. He is willing to accept Jesus' principle of forgiveness, but Peter recommends limiting that forgiveness to seven times. Peter will later walk on water in complete faith, but he will soon find himself sinking in doubt. He first refuses to let Jesus wash his feet, only to later suggest that his whole body be bathed. He swears at the Last Supper that he will stand by Jesus even when others would not. A short time later, Peter swears to a servant maid that he has never known the man named Jesus. Peter faithfully opposes the first attempts to arrest Jesus by slicing the soldier's ear. But in the end, Peter runs away to hide. In the depth of his sorrow, Jesus looks at him with loving forgiveness. Peter then goes out and weeps uncontrollably.

We have a better chance of finding out about Peter than any of the other apostles due to the fact that he is mentioned in the New Testament nearly two hundred times. This is more than the other eleven apostles combined. To learn about Peter, we look primarily in any of the four Gospels, as well as the Acts, the Letters of Paul, and the two Letters that carry the name of Peter.

So where did he come from? And when did he live? When is hard to answer. Scholars have been able to determine that he was martyred in Rome around A.D. 64, but no date of birth has ever been determined. We do know that he was born Simeon—or Simon—to his father, John, of Bethsaida. He would have been called Simeon Bar-Jona—Simon, son of John. Today we might call him Simon Johnson.

We know that he was married, because Jesus once healed Peter's mother-in-law (Mark 1:29-31). He apparently owned a successful fishing business in Capernaum—in the Northwest end of the Sea of Galilee, with his brother, Andrew. Also in this fishing partnership were James and John, the sons of Zebedee. Because Peter was in a management role in this fishing business, his leadership skills would later transfer over to his discipleship—he is often seen as the leader, the spokesman for the disciples. Every list of disciples in the New Testament mentions Peter first.

Peter has a penchant for being first. According to Mathew, Mark and Luke, he was the first one Jesus called to be a disciple. He was the first to be made a fisher of men and women. Peter was always the first to answer the Lord, no matter what question Jesus asked. According to John, Peter was the first to defend Jesus with his sword. Peter was the first disciple to enter Jesus' empty tomb. After Jesus gave him the beautiful commission to "Feed my sheep," Peter was the first to speak at Pentecost and touch three thousand souls, converting them to Christ. What is more, Peter performed the first apostolic miracle—the healing in the name of Christ of a crippled beggar (Acts 3:1-10). Not bad for a simple fisherman who always tended to speak before he thought.

Peter had the most significant role of any of the apostles. Jesus, himself, chose Peter to be the principal apostle. This might seem odd in light of Peter's predisposition for being impulsive and impetuous. Perhaps, though, the sole reason Jesus chose Peter to lead was that Peter was completely devoted to the person and the mission of Jesus.

According to the Acts of the Apostles, we know Peter was imprisoned in Jerusalem. Angels came to unlock the doors of his cell and release him. He continued to preach the message of Jesus and to be an impressive leader in the early Church. Among Catholic scholars and believers, Peter is recognized not only as an inspiring leader, but also as the first Pope in the Church hierarchy that developed.

Eventually, Peter would make his way to Rome. The Acts of the Apostles tells us he ended up in jail. This happened when many Christians were being martyred during Nero's persecutions. Again, while in jail, Peter is miraculously freed. Legend has it that at one point, as Peter was fleeing Rome to avoid martyrdom, he encountered Jesus who was walking toward Rome. "*Quo vadis, Domine?*" ("Where are you going, Master?") Peter asked. Jesus replied, "If you desert my people, I am going to Rome to be crucified a second time."

Peter understood. With that, he turned around and headed back to Rome and was eventually crucified—head down, as he did not feel worthy to be crucified in the exact way his Lord was crucified.

The exact location of Peter's tomb has been a source of debate recently. It is commonly believed, though, that the tomb is under St. Peter's Church in Vatican City, Rome.

Peter's World

What was Peter's life like before he met Jesus? We know that fishing was in his blood. Having been born in the fishing village, Bethsaida, he came by his original profession naturally. Fishing was a popular way of life for many of that time. Other jobs that would have been available at that time would have been building, agriculture, crafting and trading.[1]

We know that at one point Peter married and moved to Capernaum where he and his brother Andrew most likely owned their own commercial fishing business. But this by no means suggests that Peter was wealthy. As a matter of fact, only a very small minority was considered wealthy in that time. Only the king and his court led a sumptuous life. Most people from Peter's time were peasants; the life they led was difficult. We can imagine that this would be the case for most people in Capernaum.

Capernaum is a town in Northeastern Palestine on the Northwestern shore of the Sea of Galilee. This is the body of water where Jesus would first call Peter to be a disciple. The Sea of Galilee is also called the Lake of Galilee, since both "sea" and "lake" translate the same in both Hebrew and Greek. And truthfully, at roughly ten by fourteen miles the word *lake* seems more appropriate.[2]

Once Peter began to follow Jesus, it appears that Capernaum would become the headquarters for their ministry. To this day, we can get a very good idea of what Peter's house looked like because modern excavations have unearthed what is the very site where Peter lived. Soon after Jesus' Ascension, Peter's house in Capernaum would become a gathering place for the disciples and early Christians—a home church. There is a modern church built over the ancient house of Peter, complete with a glass floor so that visitors can look down into the exact place where the Church began.

Before all this, Peter was a Jew and his Jewish faith and heritage are important contexts for understanding him. We can assume that he lived the life of a devout Jew following the teachings of the Torah and the Law of

Moses. Peter would have worshipped in the synagogue that was located about twenty yards from his house. The synagogue is where the Jewish people of the town would gather each Sabbath to listen to the Scriptures and to pray. One constant prayer of all the Jews of that time was for a Messiah to come and free them from the oppressive rule of the Roman Empire. For at this time, all of Palestine— which held from one to two million people—was ruled by Herod the Great. This kingdom included Judea, Samaria, Galilee, Perea and some of the northern regions now a part of Syria and Jordan.[3] Herod the Great gradually built up this kingdom with a combination of political savvy and brute terror. We are told in Matthew 2:16 that it was indeed Herod who, upon hearing that a new king was to be born, ordered all male infants in Judea to be killed.[4]

The situation between the Romans and the Jews was always touch and go. The Romans found it hard to understand the rigidity of Jewish tradition and their worship of only one God,[5] and the Jews were greatly offended by the Romans' practice of polytheism— worshipping many gods.

After the death of Herod the Great, the Romans divided the kingdom and appointed Herod's sons to rule certain areas. Because Judea was the heart of the area, the Romans sent their own governor, Pontius Pilate, to govern there. Pilate would later condemn Jesus to death in Jerusalem.

What would Jerusalem have been like? Compared to Capernaum, Peter would have found Jerusalem to be quite a big city. Jerusalem—perched on a cluster of high hills—was the capital city of Israel. It was the seat of religious and political power—the trading center of Israel.[6] Some believe that Jerusalem's original name was Salem, which means peace. Peter, however, would not find peace in Jerusalem—it was not kind to those who came preaching and teaching a new way of believing.

Similar circumstances would greet Peter later in life when he went to Rome. Under the rule of Nero, Christians would face great persecutions. In the beginning of Christianity, the Roman authorities were somewhat indifferent to the new religion. That soon changed. As more and more people refused to worship the pagan gods of Rome (one of whom was sometimes the emperor), the authorities felt they had to stop them. They arrested Christians, often on trumped-up charges, sometimes even holding them responsible for natural disasters like plagues, floods, fire and famine. Peter would have to deal with this persecution later in his life.

Bethsaida, Capernaum, Jerusalem, Rome—Peter walked many lands in his life. But what would Peter have to tell us if he were walking with us today?

Notes

[1] Etienne Charpentier, *How to Read the New Testament* (New York: Crossroad Publishing Co., 1982), p. 26

[2] Carolyn Osiek, R.S.C.J., *The Bible Today*, Vol. 34, Number 3, May/June 1996.

[3] Albert J. Nevins, M.M., *The Life of Jesus Christ* (Northport, N.Y.: Costello Publishing Co., 1987), p. 16

[4] Donald Senior, *Jesus: A Gospel Portrait* (Mahwah, N.J.: Paulist Press, 1992), p. 40.

[5] Mark Link, S.J., *The Seventh Trumpet* (Niles, Ill: Argus Communications, 1978), p. 59

[6] Senior, p. 32.

DAY ONE

Growing From Sinner to Saint

Introducing Our Retreat Theme

Where do I start?

How can I, Simon Peter, possibly tell you how my whole life has changed? There is so much that has happened from the first time I met Jesus to the last time I saw him. How can I put into words the indescribable impact Jesus has had on my life?

I guess if I had to say it in only a few words, I would say it was a beautiful process—involving a difficult, yet incredible journey—of growing from sinner to saint.

As with all journeys, there is a beginning, and I would like to take you there now to have you see for yourself how Jesus called me—how he is calling all of us to join him on this journey and grow from sinner to saint.

Opening Prayer

Lord, introduce us to Peter in such a way that in coming to know him and the way he was called, we may better understand ourselves and how you are calling each of us.

Gospel Reading:

Once while Jesus was standing beside the lake of
Gennesaret, and the crowd was pressing in on him
to hear the word of God, he saw two boats there at
the shore of the lake; the fishermen had gone out
of them and were washing their nets. He got into
one of the boats, the one belonging to Simon, and
asked him to put out a little way from the shore.
Then he sat down and taught the crowds from the
boat. When he had finished speaking, he said to
Simon, "Put out into the deep water and let down
your nets for a catch." Simon answered, "Master,
we have worked all night long but have caught
nothing. Yet if you say so, I will let down the nets."
When they had done this, they caught so many
fish that their nets were beginning to break. So they
signaled their partners in the other boat to come
and help them. And they came and filled both boats,
so that they began to sink. But when Simon Peter
saw it, he fell down at Jesus' knees, saying, "Go
away from me, Lord, for I am a sinful man!" For
he and all who were with him were amazed at the
catch of fish that they had taken; and so also were
James and John, sons of Zebedee, who were partners
with Simon. Then Jesus said to Simon, "Do not be
afraid; from now on you will be catching people."
When they had brought their boats to shore, they
left everything and followed him. (Luke 5:1-11)

Retreat Session One

I remember it like it was yesterday—the day I decided
to follow the Lord.

I know there is some confusion about when I first

came to follow him. There are three different perspectives from the four Gospels. Many people ask me, "Which one is true?" I have to admit that they all are true. You see, as with any of our relationships, my relationship with Jesus did not just happen overnight. Our best relationships in life are those we develop over time. Each of the Gospels reflects this gradual, deepening devotion.

For example, the evangelist John recorded that I came to follow Jesus at the suggestion of my brother, Andrew, who was a disciple of John the Baptist.[1] Then again, some quote a retelling by both Mark and Matthew. They recount that Jesus was walking by the seashore and saw Andrew and me casting our nets. He then invited us with these words, "Follow me, and I will make you fish for people."[2]

But the story I want to share with you now is the way that Luke describes it. I feel he beautifully captured this most incredibly decisive moment in my life. And I remember it like it was yesterday.

I had this little fishing business with my brother, Andrew. Things were going pretty well in my life. Sure, there were always the Roman tax collectors that made my life complicated. They made all our lives complicated. But at least in my business, I was the boss. I was in control. I knew what I wanted. Or so I thought.

One time, I had been out fishing with my fellow fishermen all night. To say we caught nothing doesn't quite do it justice. We had come up empty every single time we had cast out our nets, all throughout the night. I didn't understand it. We had had such luck in those exact spots over and over again in the past—but not that night. We kept coming up empty.

I have to admit, I was starting to worry. You see, I had to pay those taxes to the Romans whether things were going well with my business or not. An entire night spent fishing and coming up empty, to a fisherman, is enough to make you more than uneasy.

This is when I saw him. It was Jesus of Nazareth. I knew he was a carpenter by trade and I had heard him preaching on a couple of different occasions. I have to say that he interested me a great deal even then. I knew I wanted to learn more. But on this very day when my entire fleet had caught not one fish all night, I wasn't looking for inspiration—especially from a carpenter.

But before I knew it, this carpenter—Jesus—was getting into my boat. There were other boats to choose from but he got into mine. I was not sure what to think. He instructed me to go out only slightly along the shore. Jesus sat down in my boat and continued preaching to the crowd gathered on land. His words were soothing. I sat listening to him, in somewhat of a trance. My trance was broken, though, when he was finished preaching and began to tell me how to fish.

Here I was, this seasoned fisherman with an entire fishing business and this carpenter starts telling me what to do. "Put out into deep water and let down your nets for a catch," he instructed with such a calm and knowing voice.

I was tempted to say, "And just what do you think we have been doing all night?"—but I didn't. Because the truth was my nets were empty. I had nothing.

Looking back, I realize that Jesus knew my needs better than I did. And his timing is always perfect. I guess after spending the night fishing and catching nothing, the quiet stillness of the night had led me to be reflective. In the stillness, I had started thinking about more things than just the tax collectors. I had started thinking about how in my life, I had tried to accomplish certain things and reach certain goals for myself. But I realized just how empty many of these efforts had been. There was a deep part of my life that, like the nets, was not filled. Yes. In the darkness of the night, I was able to see there was a large part of my life that was yet unfulfilled.

Isn't this the very time in all our lives when we are the most ready and willing to listen to Jesus—to let him in—not just into our boats, but into our lives? Sometimes in our lives it is emptiness, not empty nets, but the need is the same. Sometimes we are forced to face our own failures. When we have problems with marriage, career or raising a family, from time to time, no matter how hard we try, we come up empty.

This is when we are most ready to listen to the Lord—to follow him, to obey him—when we have the most need. This is also when Jesus wants to come to us the most. So he came to me. He stepped right into my boat.

That still touches me so. Jesus took the initiative and intentionally got into my boat—just as he wants to do with all of us. He is waiting to be allowed into our lives, our hearts, our minds. Every day he asks, "Will you let me in?"—it all starts or ends with that one question.

Unfortunately many get frightened by the next thing he said to me, "Put out into deep water." By saying this, he was inviting me to go deeper with him. Some honestly answer, "I don't want to go deeper. I like where I am in my life right now, no matter how shallow it may be." The Lord is always inviting us to go into deeper waters with him.

I have come to realize that this is the distinction between being a follower of Jesus and merely being a fan of his. I imagine that the Lord has many *fans*—perhaps a whole Church full of them. I wonder, though, how many *followers* he has? To truly be a follower of Jesus we have to leave behind our own plans, preferences, and priorities. We must be ready and willing to go into those unknown deep waters.

And here the Lord was in my boat, telling me that

very thing—to go into deeper waters.

That was the exact moment my life changed. Up until then, I had called the shots, I was in control. I guess you could say that, true to my given name, I had been playing, "Simon Says."

Do you remember that game? It is the one where everyone asks for permission to do something, and permission can only be granted to them if Simon says it. If Simon doesn't say it, it can't be done. I guess you could say I liked to play that game, in my life, as much as the next person. I liked having Simon be the one in control. It is only natural to want to be in control.

However, the day I listened to the Lord when he said, "Put out into deep water," was the day I stopped playing Simon Says and began to instead Follow the Leader. I was finally ready to surrender everything to the Lord.

It is a real turning point in all our lives when we are finally ready to turn to the Lord and say, "Jesus, I don't know what to do here—please help me." Usually that is a last resort. We only get to Jesus when we get to the end of our rope. It is only when we honestly turn to the Lord that we can truly turn our lives around and follow him. In order to do that, though, I had to stop doing things my way and start doing things his way. But here I am, getting ahead of myself.

You probably want to know what happened when I got into those deeper waters with Jesus on that first day. This amazes me still. As I had said, we had been out fishing all night long and had caught absolutely nothing. Truthfully, I was washing my nets, ready to quit, when Jesus got into my boat. Something inside me told me to trust him, so I actually listened when he told me to lower my net.

Instantly, the net began to pull and tug. I could tell we had caught something, but I was not prepared for what I would see next.

The net was stretched to the breaking point with every kind of fish imaginable. Never in my life had I seen such a plentiful catch. Never in my life have I experienced such fullness.

The net was so full that I had to call to my friends to come help me. My heart was racing, beating so loudly in my chest, that I couldn't even hear their responses. We began to bring in the catch, dividing it up between the two boats. Even by doing that, the weight of the catch was so great, I sincerely thought both boats could be in danger of sinking. This was only the first time of many that I would come to the beautiful realization that I was not able to contain all that the Lord was trying to give me.

That's when it hit me. That's when I realized that he knows the way to fulfillment that I have never known in my life. Jesus had enabled me to catch the fish, but in doing so, he had really caught me. That's exactly what he had been fishing for—me! Honestly, he is fishing for all of us. He wants to catch our hearts. And it is just like Jesus to use the circumstances in our very lives to catch our attention.

Overcome by this realization, I did something very uncharacteristic. I fell to my knees at the feet of Jesus. It seems to me that when we truly begin to experience the Lord in our lives, it indeed puts us on our knees. It humbles us. It makes us aware of who we are and who the Lord is. We recognize that we do not deserve what he is offering us. When we finally recognize how blessed we are, it often leads us to our knees. Besides this feeling of unworthiness, I fell to my knees with the overwhelming sense of Jesus' goodness.

And while on my knees, the only thing I could manage to say was, "Go away from me, Lord, for I am a sinful man."

That wasn't like me either. I was always so full of
confidence. And I really didn't feel I was a bad person.
But there is something about standing in the light of the
Lord that illuminates all of the shadows in our souls. This
incredible light makes us painfully aware of our own
darkness and sinfulness.

Isn't it ironic that sometimes the very thing we are
seeking is the very thing we shy away from, especially
with the Lord? You have to understand that I didn't use
the title "Lord" without reason. My bursting heart told
me this was my Lord.

It would not be the last time I would be brought to
my knees, but it is a time I will never forget. I could feel
the love of Jesus pouring forth, filling the place in my
heart that I didn't even know was empty. I couldn't help
but feel unworthy, so I told him to leave me.

But, as always, Jesus knows best. He saw my fear
and replied, "Do not be afraid; from now on you will be
catching people."

I had not learned enough yet to know what that
meant, but I had learned enough to know I could trust
the Lord with my life. At that moment, I couldn't have
known that years later, on the feast of Pentecost, I would
be blessed to bring in to the Church three thousand new
Christian men and women. Once again, it wasn't because
of me, but because I followed Jesus' direction and his
spirit.

Of course, I still had many questions. Why did he
choose me? I understood why I might need Jesus in my
life, but I could not understand why he needed me. I
could think of several other people right off the top of my
head who were better than I was. So why would he want
me? What would I be doing? I had no idea what I was
being called to do. I knew that rabbis would often take in
students and teach them the Torah—the law. I did not yet

understand that Jesus was not calling me to learn a law, but to learn a life. I did not understand much at all. But that was the day I was ready to trust.

We brought our bulging boats into shore and decided these gifts were meant to be shared. The crowd was still gathered there, absolutely amazed—not by anything I had done, but by what the Lord had brought about. At that point, I decided to leave everything and become his follower.

Now don't assume that this meant I abandoned my family. No, I simply tried to give up all that would keep me from sincerely following Jesus. I tried to give up my own ego. I tried to give up my control. I tried to give up my preoccupation with being successful. I left behind the way I had been living my life thus far and I began to allow the Lord to lead me where he wanted me to go. I was being asked to completely change my priorities. I would now need to put the Lord first in my life. There was no doubt about it. I was on my way to becoming a new man.

The story doesn't end there. My journey from sinner to saint had just begun. I went into deeper waters with the Lord because he got into my boat. He called me to follow him. I remember it like it was yesterday.

Today, Jesus wants to get into your boat—your life— your heart. He is calling you now, inviting you to enter into a deeper relationship with him.

For Reflection

- *Can you identify any areas of loneliness, neediness or emptiness in your life that are waiting to be filled?*

- *Can you see how these very areas of need might be a way for Jesus to enter into your life just as he entered into*

Peter's boat, only after he had experienced emptiness?

■ *In what specific way do you feel Jesus calling you to follow him? In doing this, what might he be asking you to let go of?*

Closing Prayer

"Here I Am, Lord"

Here I am, Lord
Is it I, Lord?
I have heard You
   calling in the night
I will go, Lord
If You lead me
I will hold Your people
   in my heart.[3]

Notes

[1] See John 1:40-42.

[2] See Matthew 4:18-22 and Mark 1:16-20.

[3] "Here I Am, Lord" Dan Schutte, OCP Publications.

Day Two
Walking in Faith

Coming Together in the Spirit

Reflections by Father Jim

Walking in faith. Just as Peter realized, I have realized that those are easy words to say, but so very hard to live.

You see, I have stage four renal cell cancer. As someone who lives with the turbulence of cancer, I am learning every day how utterly imperative it is for us to do just that—walk in faith.

Many times, I find myself stepping out in faith as I begin my days. Granted, it is not that surprising to hear a priest say that. Then along comes a discouraging doctor's visit, a saddening statistic, or the sickening side effects of various treatments and I can honestly feel my inner spirit sinking. But before I drown in these doubts and worries, I find myself crying out to the Lord for help. He saves me every time.

I only have to remember to keep my eyes on him, place all my trust in him. By holding onto Jesus, I can rise above any anxiety that comes my way. By holding onto Jesus, I am able to walk in faith and find complete peace. By God's amazing grace, I am learning how to walk on water by walking in faith.

This is exactly the lesson Peter was learning in the following Gospel story. He was learning how important it is to always keep your eyes on the Lord to keep from becoming overwhelmed by the frightening forces that come against us. Should we forget this and take our eyes off him, all we need do is call out for him and he will be there.

Opening Prayer

Lord, may you open our minds and hearts and our souls to understand and to live the words of the Holy Gospel so that we may truly walk in faith.

Gospel Reading:

Immediately [Jesus] made the disciples get into the boat and go on ahead to the other side, while he dismissed the crowds. And after he had dismissed the crowds, he went up the mountain by himself to pray. When evening came, he was there alone, but by this time the boat, battered by the waves, was far from the land, for the wind was against them. And early in the morning he came walking toward them on the sea. But when the disciples saw him walking on the sea, they were terrified, saying, "It is a ghost!" And they cried out in fear. But immediately Jesus spoke to them and said, "Take heart, it is I; do not be afraid."

Peter answered him, "Lord, if it is you, command me to come to you on the water." He said, "Come." So Peter got out of the boat, started walking on the water, and came toward Jesus. But when he noticed the strong wind, he became frightened, and beginning to sink, he cried out, "Lord, save me!" Jesus immediately reached out his hand and caught him, saying to him, "You of little faith, why did you doubt?" When they got into the boat, the wind ceased. And those in the boat worshipped him,

saying, "Truly you are the Son of God."
(Matthew 14:22-33)

Retreat Session Two

Everything Jesus does is for a reason.

Every movement, every spoken word goes much deeper than what we usually understand. The many miracles he performed often have more meaning than we realize. As a disciple, I was blessed to witness Jesus perform many miracles. I feel even more blessed that I never ceased to be amazed.

Of all the magnificent miracles I witnessed, one that is forever in my heart and my mind is the one I want to tell you about now. It had been a trying day for Jesus. He had just received the news about the death of John the Baptist and had wanted to go off somewhere and pray. Of course, by this time, he was becoming quite a celebrity. People were always following him. In the midst of his prayer time, he realized a crowd had come to hear him preach and ask for healings. As always, he came to those who had come to him. He spoke and healed and touched many hearts.

When it started to get dark, we suggested to him that he should dismiss the crowd so that they could get to the nearby towns in order to eat before it got too late. But, as usual, Jesus had a better plan.

This is when he proceeded to feed the crowd of over five thousand, with only five loaves of bread and two fish. Imagine that! It was, indeed, an amazing miracle.[1]

What happened next is even more astounding to me. Jesus told us disciples to get into the boat and begin to head to the other side, while he dismissed the well-fed crowd for the night. He also mentioned he wanted to be alone to continue his time of prayer.

The last time I saw him that night, we were in our small boat while he was heading up to a mountainside to pray. Once in our boat, we continued to talk excitedly about the miracle we had just witnessed. Five loaves of bread and two fish! Jesus fed over five thousand hungry people with this and even had enough left over to feed more! We were so caught up in our conversation that the storm took us completely by surprise.

It seemed to come from out of nowhere. The winds of this storm were as violent as any I had seen in my days as a fisherman. We could not control our boat. I have to admit, I was more frightened than I can ever remember being. I kept thinking, "Is this how it's going to end?" I could not figure out what to do. I started to call out, "Jesus, where are you?"

I remember wondering why he wouldn't come the moment I asked. I wondered where he was when I needed him. Why did he have us get in this little boat after all?

Of course, my fears were magnified even more because the night was pitch black. Usually I could adjust my vision to the light of the moon, but on that night, the moon was covered by the clouds. Isn't it true that in the darkness, all of our problems seem more ominous and overwhelming?

I needed to do something, but I didn't know what. Then, I remembered what Jesus had taught us the day he went up on a mountain shortly after facing forty days in the desert. With all of us disciples gathered around him, he began teaching us so much that day. I cannot say I understood all of it—there was so much to remember. It was as if he was giving us many sermons on that mountain. One thing I do remember is that he taught us how to pray.

> Pray then in this way: Our Father in heaven,
> hallowed be your name. Your kingdom come. Your
> will be done, on earth as it is in heaven. Give us
> this day our daily bread. And forgive us our debts,
> as we also have forgiven our debtors. And do not
> bring us to the time of trial, but rescue us from the
> evil one.[2]

I tried to pray the way Jesus had taught us. I was surprised to realize it helped. Still, I so badly needed him to come to us.

I have no idea how long we were out there, but finally there was a break in the darkness. I saw the sun begin to rise. At that very moment, I saw what I felt was certainly a ghost. I thought I might be seeing things. But upon hearing the screams of my companions, I realized they saw this figure, too. It was then that he spoke. "Take heart, it is I; do not be afraid."

Isn't that just like the Lord? He is always trying to calm our fears. I cannot recall how many times those words of Jesus have soothed my pain, whether physical or mental. He tells us all, "Take heart, it is I; do not be afraid."

Never had I felt such utter relief! I was so happy to see the Lord—to know he answered my prayer—that at first, I did not even realize that he was walking on water. He was walking on water!

Jesus could have gotten to us in many ways. Why would he choose to walk across the water? Was it just something he hadn't tried yet and decided to do? Was it the shortest route to take? But, as I said earlier, everything Jesus does is for a purpose—the greater good. Maybe he was reminding me then that God can do anything. He has divine power over the worldly forces. God has control over the weather, the water and whatever else might threaten us.

But right then all I understood was that he was walking on water!

Upon recognizing him and what he was doing, I said something to him that even now, I can't believe I said. "Lord, if it is you, command me to come to you on the water."

You may be wondering what on earth I was thinking! Truthfully, I have wondered that myself. Having thought it through many times since trying to answer that question, I have come to the conclusion that having been so frightened in the small boat, enduring those bitter winds that battered us about, I was in a dark place. And just like so many times in our lives when life seems the darkest, the rising Son brings us hope.

I was ecstatic to see my Savior walking toward me at that moment. I wanted not only to be with him, but also I wanted to be like him. I, too, wanted to walk on water. Now, I wouldn't have blamed Jesus at all if he had simply responded to my request by saying, "Peter, you know you can't do the things I do." Instead, believe it or not, he said, "Come." Jesus was telling me that all things are possible with him. All we have to do is ask. Without a second thought, I started to get out of the boat. It did occur to me that none of the others were climbing overboard with me. It was just me. It was just like me to be so impetuous.

I think my heart actually leapt into my mouth when I realized I was out of the boat and I was walking across the water toward my Lord. I was stepping out in faith and walking on the water!

For a moment, I wasn't afraid. The Lord was teaching me that faith makes fear disappear. But, as always, I still had so much to learn. As it often happens in life, such faithful confidence didn't last. No sooner had I begun to walk across the water than I became frighteningly aware of the elements around me. The winds and the waves were pounding all over me. The pelting water stung my face in such a furious fashion that I could no longer see. My body grew cold. I started to shiver uncontrollably. I became aware that I was sinking.

This, too, I came to understand, is what happens to all of us. So often we are doing well in our faith. But when we are faced with the winds and the waves of worry, we sink. I knew I could not survive on my own. For when we rely just on ourselves, we are soon in way over our heads.

I had two choices. I could cry out to the Lord for help. Or I could sink in the storm. This may seem like an easy choice, but it's not. Too many times, we choose to futilely struggle on our own instead of simply calling out to the Lord.

Thankfully, this time I did the only thing that could possibly save me. I cried out to the Lord for help. As always, the Lord was there for me. His strong and loving hand reached out for me—as it reaches out for all of us—and he saved me. Holding on to his protective hand, I again, felt so overjoyed. I had walked on water! I wondered if Jesus was as excited about that fact as I was. Then he said it. "You of little faith, why did you doubt?"

Now, *that* got my attention. I was hoping he might say, "Wow! You were really doing great for a while." Or maybe he would say, "Peter, you are so brave. None of the others dared to try what you did." But instead, Jesus cuts right to the heart of the matter. "You of little faith, why did you doubt?" And I understood.

It was by faith and by faith alone that I could rise above the elements—walk on water. But as soon as I felt the winds and waves against me, I began to sink with doubt. It was my shallow faith that almost sunk me into the deep waters. But Jesus saved me. All I had to do was ask him.

When we got back to the boat, I realized the bitter wind had now been calmed, both outwardly and inwardly. Then, all at once, all in the boat gathered around Jesus and began to worship him with the words, "Truly you are the Son of God."

One of the beautiful Psalms—I believe it is Psalm 107—immediately flooded my heart and my mind. "Then they cried to the Lord in their trouble, and he brought them out from their distress; he made the storm be still, and the waves of the sea were hushed. Then they were glad because they had quiet, and he brought them to their desired haven."[3]

Everything Jesus does is for a reason. I cannot tell you the number of times in my life that recalling that very incident helped me through an otherwise impossible situation. Jesus had to teach me that if I can keep my eyes on him, no matter what the winds, the waves, and the world are doing to me, I can get through it. And there is no greater strength to be found than when we call out his name.

I realized that even when the waves were battering our little boat and I felt momentarily abandoned, that Jesus was still hearing me. He was praying for me. The experience in that little boat would help me years later when the infant Church, so small against the bigger elements of the Roman Empire, would be battered about in a violent storm of controversy and oppression. Like in the boat, the Church would constantly be working against a force that was overwhelming. But just like on that day on the sea, years later, I would again find my peace with the rising of the Son.

Everything Jesus does is for a reason. And while we may not always know that reason, Jesus does want us all to know that everything he does is for us. He is there for all of us. When the storms of life seem to batter us the hardest, it is natural to feel alone. But we must simply remember to call out his name.

Even when we are sinking, failing at something, the Lord is there for us. We just have to call out his name and keep our eyes on him. Once we learn how to walk on water by walking in faith, we will never walk alone.

For Reflection

- *Can you recall turbulent times in your life—how you felt and how you responded to those situations?*

- *Recall a time when you stepped out in faith. What happened as a result?*

- *Can you remember any time in your life when you were drowning in doubts, falling into fear, sinking into depression? Did you call out to the Lord for help by praying?*

Closing Prayer

"You'll Never Walk Alone"

When you walk through a storm
    keep your head up high
And don't be afraid of the dark.
At the end of the storm is a
    golden sky
And the sweet, simple song of
    the lark.
Walk on through the wind
Walk on through the rain
Though your dreams be tossed
    and blown.

Walk on, walk on
With hope in your heart
And you'll never walk alone
You'll never walk alone.[4]

Notes

[1] See Matthew 14:13-21.

[2] See Matthew 6:9.

[3] See Psalms 107:28-30.

[4] "You'll Never Walk Alone," *Carousel*, lyrics by Oscar Hammerstein II.

DAY THREE
Recognizing Who We Are

Coming Together in the Spirit

Reflections by Father Jim

Every day when I feel I am struggling with one of the many difficulties of having cancer, I feel the Lord tell me, just as he told Peter and the other disciples, "If any want to become my followers, let them deny themselves and take up their cross and follow me."[1]

It helps me to remember those words.

And it also helps me to remember the words of another man who picked up his cross and beautifully followed Jesus. A dear man to whom I refer as my spiritual father, Cardinal Joseph Bernardin, was Archbishop of Chicago. While in the midst of his own cancer battle, he gave the following message in one of his homilies:

> My spiritual journey goes back for many years. But it did not really begin to take shape until I learned, with my heart as well as my mind, who Jesus is and what he expects of me. The answers to these two questions came over a period of time through study of the Scriptures, prayer, exchanges with my fellow priests, and my ministerial experiences, but especially through prayer and the Scriptures. It is both the discovery and the internalization of the answers to those two questions that have given me

the strength to carry the cross that Jesus has given me the privilege to share with him.

Peter soon discovers the impact that these same questions will have on his life. And these two questions are deeply connected. For it is only after we discover who Jesus is for us that we can completely understand what it is that Jesus expects of us. Without understanding who Jesus is, there is no way we can begin to pick up our own cross and follow him.

The strength that comes from knowing Jesus and what he expects from us was meant to empower Peter to go where it was Jesus was leading. The same is true for us all.

Opening Prayer

Lord, come to us today through the words of your Holy Gospel and the words of your disciple Peter, so that we can truly know who you are.

Gospel Reading:

Now when Jesus came into the district of Caesarea Philippi, he asked his disciples, "Who do people say that the Son of Man is?" And they said, "Some say John the Baptist, but others Elijah, and still others Jeremiah or one of the prophets." He said to them, "But who do you say that I am?" Simon Peter answered, "You are the Messiah, the Son of the living God." And Jesus answered him, "Blessed are you, Simon son of Jonah! For flesh and blood has not revealed this to you, but my Father in heaven. And I tell you, you are Peter, and on this rock I will build my church, and the gates of Hades will not prevail against it. I will give you the keys of the kingdom of heaven, and whatever you bind on earth will be bound in heaven, and whatever you

loose on earth will be loosed in heaven." Then he
sternly ordered the disciples not to tell anyone that
he was the Messiah. From that time on, Jesus began
to show his disciples that he must go to Jerusalem
and undergo great suffering at the hands of the
elders and chief priests and scribes, and be killed,
and on the third day be raised. And Peter took him
aside and began to rebuke him, saying, "God forbid
it, Lord! This must never happen to you." But he
turned and said to Peter, "Get behind me, Satan! You
are a stumbling block to me; for you are setting your
mind not on divine things but on human things."
Then Jesus told his disciples, "If any want to become
my followers, let them deny themselves and take up
their cross and follow me. For those who want to
save their life will lose it, and those who lose their
life for my sake will find it. For what will it profit
them if they gain the whole world but forfeit their
life? Or what will they give in return for their life?
For the Son of Man is to come with his angels in the
glory of his Father, and then he will repay everyone
for what has been done." (Matthew 16:13-27)

RETREAT SESSION THREE

"Who do you say that I am?"

When I answered that question for Jesus, it changed
more for me than just my name. But before you respond
to that question, let me tell you a little more about that day.

I remember how much I was looking forward to
traveling to the area of Caesarea Philippi—twenty-five
miles north of Capernaum, where I used to own my
fishing business. When Jesus told us about it, I thought
it would be good for Jesus and all of us disciples, to get

away together and spend some time in prayer.

Things had been a little stressful. Because Jesus' popularity was growing every day, the people in power were getting suspicious. The Pharisees and Sadducees had even come to him to test him and demand a sign from heaven. When Jesus did not oblige them, they became incredibly upset.[2]

I assumed this was one of the things he felt drawn to pray about when we arrived. But, as usual, I didn't know the half of it.

Jesus called all of us together and began by asking us, "Who do people say that the Son of Man is?" Now, I had heard him refer to himself before as "the Son of Man," so I knew at least that he was talking about himself. That intrigued me. Why would Jesus be interested in what people said about him? It occurred to me that he might simply want to know where he stood with people.

But how could he not know? Everywhere we went, Jesus would draw a crowd. He would teach and touch these people like no one had ever seen before. And then there were the miracles! Everywhere we went, we left the crowd spellbound and wanting more.

Wouldn't Jesus already know what people were saying about him?

At the time I didn't understand why he would ask this. But later I began to suspect that Jesus was struggling with that very question about who he was, himself. I have heard it said that to understand our identity, to a large extent, determines our destiny. It is only after we understand who we are that we can come close to understanding where we are going.

We all somewhat began talking at the same time when Jesus asked that. Because of all the wonderful things he had done, the rumors were flying. Some thought he was John the Baptist, who had just recently been killed. Others were sure he was Elijah, a prophet from the Old Testament who rode off in a flaming chariot to heaven.[3] Still others speculated that he was Jeremiah or another prophet. It was clear that while people may not have understood who Jesus was, they were already aware that he was someone important.

I thought Jesus might just take those answers and ponder them a while. But, as I've already shared with you, Jesus always wants to go deeper.

"But who do you say that I am?"

Now, I realized he was not just speaking to me, he was asking this question of all of us. But, somehow over the course of the months we had all been together, I had taken on the role of spokesman for the disciples. I would have liked to think that it had to do with a great leadership quality that I possess, but I suspect it had more to do with the fact that I was simply the most outspoken one.

Only this time what came out of my mouth surprised even me. "You are the Messiah, the Son of the living God."

Where did that come from? All of us disciples had been so amazed at this man we had grown to love. The many miracles proved this was no normal human being. But I have to confess that I had never before come to the conclusion that he was, indeed, the Messiah—the Son of God.

For once, though, my tendency to speak out was a good thing. Even Jesus was quite impressed. "Blessed are you, Simon son of Jonah! For flesh and blood has not revealed this to you, but my Father in heaven."

I don't know if I can fully describe what that meant to me to hear that. Jesus was confirming and affirming so much for me with that one statement. So, it was true! Jesus *is* the Son of God. And God had revealed this to me! I was overjoyed!

Looking back, this moment is one of the most

significant moments of my life. What a blessing it is for all of us to know who Jesus is!

It was true! My mind was racing with this new information. Just imagine what Jesus, the Son of God, could do! Israel has been waiting for him for so long. The world has been waiting for him for so long!

I think this would have been enough information for me to become overwhelmed, but Jesus kept astounding me as he continued.

> And I tell you, you are Peter, and on this rock I will build my church, and the gates of Hades will not prevail against it. I will give you the keys of the kingdom of heaven, and whatever you bind on earth will be bound in heaven, and whatever you loose on earth will be loosed in heaven.

Jesus just said he was giving me the keys of the kingdom of heaven! Now, I understood about how great kings had porters whom they entrusted with the keys to their palaces, but was my Master now telling me he was giving me the original Master key? Was Jesus making me the steward of the Kingdom of God?

Honestly, though, I didn't have time to think about that part of what Jesus said, because the first part was still echoing too loudly in my head. "And I tell you, you are Peter..."

He changed my name! He never changed the name of anyone else. But he changed my name. Jesus knew that I was changing, too. My new name would mean *rock*. And it was no coincidence that he then said "...and on this rock I will build my church, and the gates of Hades will not prevail against it."

I had to wonder what that meant. Was Jesus telling me that I was the rock upon which he would build the Church? Was he telling me that my faith was the rock?

Maybe he was referring to himself as the rock? Or was the rock that the Church would be built upon simply referring to the truth that Jesus was the Messiah?

But it didn't matter what it all meant. Jesus had just given me a new name that meant "rock" and if Jesus thought I was a strong rock, I would become one for him. I would do anything for the Messiah. He had just handed me the keys to the Kingdom of God! The Messiah had made me his right hand man!

Jesus is the Messiah! I could not wait to share this news with everyone I knew! But then, he told us not to say a word.

At first I was stunned. Why wouldn't we want to shout this news from every mountaintop in the world? Everyone should know that our Messiah had come. My old business knowledge was kicking in at this time. I started planning! If we could draw a crowd before, one can only imagine the crowds that would now want to come. We could fill stadiums full of cheering people all wanting to see the Messiah who had finally come.

Granted, when people talked about the Messiah coming, most of us expected a great military hero or political ruler or great king, and Jesus didn't fit those images. It would be a long time before I would fully understand that the Messiah was to usher in the reign of the greatest king of all—he would usher in God's reign—where peace and justice would prevail.

While I didn't understand all of this at that very moment, I still so badly wanted others to know the Messiah had come!

As always Jesus was looking at the big picture while all I could see was what was in front of my face. He knew all too well what other people expected a Messiah to be. He knew all too well what the people like the Pharisees and Sadducees would do with this information. Jesus knew all too well what was going to happen to him.

This next part hurts me still. Repeating it today is like hearing it for the first time. Jesus—the Messiah—the one who had come to save us all, started telling us what was going to happen to him. He said he must go into Jerusalem where he would suffer greatly, be killed, and be raised on the third day. Truthfully, I don't think I fully heard the part about being raised, or I would have asked him to explain that one immediately. But I had heard him say he had to suffer and be killed.

This was the first time any of us had ever heard about this. You have to understand that this man was more than a dear friend to me. He was my Lord. I wanted to follow him everywhere. I could not stand the thought of him suffering, let alone dying. To be honest, I could not stand the thought of myself suffering and dying either. I had to speak up, but I didn't want to do so in front of the others. I pulled him aside and quietly advised him, "God forbid it, Lord! This must never happen to you."

His reaction to this comment did more than startle me. "Get behind me, Satan! You are a stumbling block to me; for you are setting your mind not on divine things but on human things." This crushed my pride!

Wasn't he just telling me how divinely inspired I was? Didn't he just change my name to indicate the "rock" upon which he would build his Church? How had I gone from a rock to a stumbling block in such a short period of time?

Much later I would come to understand that part of Jesus' intense reaction was due to his own inner struggle. I had just given voice to the very thoughts with which the devil had earlier been tempting Jesus. Had I fully understood who Jesus was, I could have offered him the support he needed. Instead, I only offered him more seeds of doubt.

"Who do you say that I am?" he had asked me.
Though I answered as if I knew who he was, I guess I
didn't fully understand. It is easy to say we believe in
Jesus. But do we believe enough?

We need to open our eyes, minds, and hearts to see
Jesus as he truly is—in his own true light. Only then can
we begin to see ourselves and what he expects of us—in
this same light of the Lord.

But at that moment, I couldn't see the light. I only
saw the darkness. Jesus really got this point across to me
when he called me Satan. What a tumble that was for me!
I had been feeling so elated when Jesus blessed me for
what I said about him being the Son of the living God.
And yet, when I went with that same instinct to speak up
the second time, it greatly humbled me.

Isn't that true for us all?

One moment we can be really inspired and the next
moment, we are really off-track. One minute we feel
positively under the influence of God, and the next
minute, we are under the influence of the evil one. We
need to be aware that at any time in life, it is possible for
us to be pulled in either direction by either force. That
day, I became so incredibly conscious of my strengths
and my weaknesses and how present they are within me
at the same time. That is how I could be both a rock of
strength and yet a stumbling block. Sometimes the spirit
we are following is holy and sometimes it is not holy at all.

Unfortunately, it would not be the last time that I
would be under the influence of the evil one. But all I
could focus on right then was that Jesus was telling me
that he was to suffer and die. He was telling me who
he was. And then he told me who he wanted me to be.
"If any want to become my followers, let them deny
themselves and take up their cross and follow me. For
those who want to save their life will lose it, and those

who lose their life for my sake will find it."

I have to admit I didn't understand completely what that meant for a long time. But even then I did understand that being a follower of Jesus was not going to be easy. I had thought it was going to be so different.

I had so many questions I wanted to ask. And I, of course, had so many suggestions I wanted to make: Couldn't we discuss this? Couldn't he save the world at a less costly price?

I was so confused! I had given up everything to follow the Lord when he invited me to follow him. And now he was telling me things about the future that I didn't want to know. Later on, I would let him know my childish thoughts and fears. Because one of the next times Jesus would speak of the future, I would blurt out, "Look, we have left everything and followed you. What then will we have?" (Matthew 19:27) This wasn't at all what I had dreamed of. It wasn't my plan in the least.

I guess, when any of us dream, we dream of a perfect life. We have these great plans for what that life will be. And when things don't go according to our hopes and dreams, we want to yell, "Time out! Lord, this isn't at all in my plan." And the Lord must want to tell us, "But it's part of my plan."

How true it is that we can't see things the way God does. I think Isaiah quotes the Lord best about this when he records, "For as the heavens are higher than the earth, so are my ways higher than your ways and my thoughts than your thoughts."[4]

I understood that God's ways are so far above my ways, but it would be much later before I realized how significant that day was to my spiritual growth. I was, indeed, at a crossroads in my life. For in the course of that day I had to answer two questions that would set my spiritual path forever. I had to answer who Jesus was to me and what Jesus expected from me.

I thought I had already answered that first question on the day I left my fishing nets and began to follow him. But I realize now that at that time I was solely committed to my own vision of Jesus. Now, I had to be committed to the Lord's vision of himself and me.

And that made that last question even harder to answer. It was so difficult to realize that he had chosen the way of the cross. And as his follower—if I was to be true to my word—I had to follow him there.

Wouldn't it be nice if we could achieve the same results without sacrificing so much? But we can't. Jesus isn't looking for part-time followers. He is asking for a full-time commitment from each of us.

What does Jesus expect from you? But before you can answer that question, you need to think long and hard about what you would say if Jesus came to you today, looked you in the eyes and said: "Who do you say that I am?"

For Reflection

- *Who is Jesus for you today?*

- *Who are you in terms of your relationship to the Lord?*

- *What stumbling blocks in your life trip you the most on your spiritual path?*

- *Can you recall times when you were under the influence of the evil spirit, and times when you were under the influence of the Holy Spirit?*

Closing Prayer

"Day By Day"

Day by day
Day by day
Oh, Dear Lord, three
     things I pray
To see Thee more clearly,
Love Thee more dearly,
Follow Thee more nearly,
Day by day.[5]

Notes

[1] See Matthew 16:24.

[2] See Matthew 16:1-4.

[3] See 2 Kings 2:11.

[4] See Isaiah 55:9.

[5] "Day by Day," *Godspell*, music and lyrics by Stephen Schwartz.

DAY FOUR

Reaching the Heights of Holiness

Coming Together in the Spirit

Reflections by Father Jim

One of the things I struggle with the most with having a terminal disease is dealing with all the incredible disappointments. I am convinced, though, that God gives us insight—he gives us vision—that will see us through the many hard times to come. This is what happened to me.

Once after a particularly difficult doctor visit, where I was told that the horribly debilitating chemotherapy I had just endured had not worked to curb my cancer, I was devastated. But immediately upon receiving this news, I was given a thought that I had not remembered for a long time. Several months earlier, there had been a healing service at my parish. During this service, I asked Jesus to heal me and I truly believe the Lord spoke these words to me, "I will give you length of days to fulfill this great mission I have given you on earth." At once, I knew these were not my words, they had to have come to me from somewhere else.

While this comforted me at that time, I hadn't thought of the healing service or that beautiful vision for months, but at that moment of despair in the doctor's office, when

I needed it the most, the Lord reminded me of it. To this day, that vision gives me comfort by reminding me that I may not know what my future holds, but I know who holds my future.

Peter is about to have a vision that will transform his life. This mountaintop experience will give him a bright outlook on the future that had earlier frightened him to death. He will be better able to deal with the earlier "death sentence" Jesus predicted.

These mountaintop moments—times when you feel so close to the Lord—happen today in private prayer, intimate moments with family and friends, conferences, missions, and retreats as well. The Lord wants to share with all of us a vision of what we can be, a vision of what his love offers us.

Opening Prayer

Lord, lead us to the mountain of revelation, so that we can see and experience for ourselves, all that you want to share with us.

Gospel Reading:

Six days later, Jesus took with him Peter and James and his brother John and led them up a high mountain, by themselves. And he was transfigured before them, and his face shone like the sun, and his clothes became dazzling white. Suddenly there appeared to them Moses and Elijah, talking with him. Then Peter said to Jesus, "Lord, it is good for us to be here; if you wish, I will make three dwellings here, one for you, one for Moses, and one for Elijah." While he was still speaking, suddenly a bright cloud overshadowed them, and from the cloud a voice said, "This is my Son, the Beloved; with him I am well pleased; listen to him!" When the disciples heard this, they fell to the ground and were overcome by fear. But Jesus came and touched them, saying, "Get up and do not be afraid." And when they looked up, they saw no one except Jesus himself alone. As they were coming down the mountain, Jesus ordered them, "Tell no one about the vision until after the Son of Man has been raised from the dead." (Matthew 17:1-9)

Retreat Session Four

The climb was pretty steep.

Of course, I think I was climbing while still in a state of shock. It had only been six days since my world had changed. It had been six days since I answered to Jesus that he was the Son of God. It had been six days since he informed me for the first time about his approaching passion, death and resurrection. And I confess that as much as I was struggling to reach the top of the mountain, I was also greatly struggling with what I had just learned, trying hard to reach an understanding of it all.

That is why I was so glad that Jesus suggested a bit of a retreat for us all to go away and pray for awhile. I did wonder why the others weren't invited to come along, but I felt so honored that he would invite James and John and me to join him, that I didn't think too long about the rest. Already I sensed that this time together would be very special.

And so we began to climb one of the highest mountains in Palestine, Mount Tabor. Jesus, of course, led the way.

Climbing the mountain wasn't easy. The ascent was

difficult. I was so tempted to stop several times along the way and say, "I'm tired. This spot is good enough." But Jesus, as always, kept leading us to a higher place.

So many times in my life after that moment, I wanted to stop what I was doing because I thought it was "good enough." I had reached a level in my life that seemed quite adequate. But just like that day, I could feel the Lord keep saying, "No, that's not enough. Keep on climbing. I want to lead you to greater heights."

Now, Jesus is not one for small talk, so that day we climbed in silence. For once, I did not mind being quiet. The peaceful beauty of the mountainside was awe-inspiring. I felt as if we were climbing to where the earth meets up with heaven.

There is just something so sacred about a mountain. I started thinking about how mountains in the Bible are such sacred sites. I thought of Moses receiving the Ten Commandments on Mount Sinai. I started thinking of Elijah who experienced the Lord's presence on Mount Horeb. Little did I know how ironic those thoughts would be when we finally got to where we were going.

At last, we reached the top. To describe it as breathtaking probably does not do it justice. I was so grateful we hadn't quit before we reached our destination. I was struck by how different my view was from the top of the mountain, than it had been down at the bottom. While standing a thousand feet above Galilee, that which seemed quite large down below, from the mountain, was but a speck. I suspected this was a glimpse at the majesty of God and the smallness of our problems. On the mountain, I had a better perspective of God's point of view. I had no idea how significant this insight was.

While I had been looking down, marveling at the view from the top of the mountain, Jesus, of course, was still looking higher. When I turned around, I noticed he was looking up. Already he seemed enraptured in the presence of God. I wondered if the news of his coming suffering and death, that had been so hard for me to come to terms with, was laying heavy on Jesus' heart as well.

And what happened next, I could hardly believe. Before my very eyes, Jesus began to shine like the sun. Now, I had heard the terms "radiant" and "glowing" used to describe people before, but I had never fully known what they meant until that very moment. Jesus was emanating a light from within him that ordinarily would have made me need to shield my eyes from its intensity. But this time, I could not look away. His clothes were the whitest of whites—and after a day of mountain climbing, that, itself, was quite incredible. I could not take my eyes off him. I could not even turn away from this sight to see if John and James were seeing what I was seeing. I didn't want to miss a moment. Truly, I was watching the Son of the living God. I could, indeed, feel the Spirit of the living God all around me.

Just as this was sinking in, they appeared. At first I thought I was seeing angels appearing to Jesus and talking to him. But then I knew. In that way you know something, even though you have no idea how you know it—I knew who they were! Maybe it was because I had just been thinking about them both while climbing the mountain. But clear as day, I knew that the two angels were none other than Moses and Elijah!

Moses and Elijah!

Two of the greatest men in Israel's history were standing next to my Lord. Moses, who represented the Law, and Elijah, who represented the prophets, were standing next to the one who had come to fulfill both the law and prophets. Jesus would complete the circle.

Moses, Elijah and Jesus, the Son of God, were standing in front of me, talking! And I was standing there, taking it all in. A wise man would have simply bowed down in silence at this majestic sight. I, quite typically, spoke up. "Lord, it is good for us to be here; if you wish, I will make three dwellings here, one for you, one for Moses, and one for Elijah."

Many would later ask me what I was thinking. Honestly, I'm not sure. I think I said this partly because I did not want that moment to ever end. I wanted that mountaintop experience to go on and on. I was so incredibly moved and humbled by it all that I wanted to build the three of them monuments on that very site so that it would always be seen as the sacred site it was. But before my final word was out of my trembling mouth, the cloud came.

Now, as a fisherman, I was always very good at reading the clouds. I could tell with a glance what kind of weather we would be having by the type of clouds I saw. But I had never in my life seen a cloud like this one. Just as white as Jesus' clothes were, this cloud was also as bright. It came directly over us and I heard a voice boom forth. "This is my Son, the Beloved; with him I am well pleased; listen to him!"

Over the last several months, I had begun to expect the unexpected. But that was beyond compare. I fell to the ground. I believe I was just so overwhelmed by the presence of God that I had no choice but to fall to the ground, completely awestruck. Never in my life had I experienced such a profound sense of God's presence.

I cannot tell you just how long we were on the ground. Time, as I had known it, did not seem to matter anymore. But there we were, humbled and trembling, when Jesus came over to us. "Get up and do not be afraid."

How many times he had told me, "Do not be afraid"! How many times he would tell me that again and again! Those words brought me great peace. When I looked up, it was only Jesus standing there. I quickly looked all around me, but all that remained on that mountain was Jesus, James, John and I.

Jesus looked so peaceful. I realized that he himself had experienced something profound. While he was not radiating the same light he had earlier, there was an afterglow that remained in him that I had not seen before. He truly looked like a man who could face whatever the future held for him. And I truly felt like a man who could face whatever was to come, with him.

At the time, I did not understand why I suddenly felt so confident in the future. Later I would realize that God had just given us a vision of how Jesus would appear for all eternity, after he entered into his glory. It was such an incredible vision of absolute magnificence that I was no longer afraid. I had been blessed with a vision that I felt privileged to share.

I still didn't understand it all, but for once, I felt I didn't need to understand. Then, Jesus raised us up from the ground as he said to us, "Tell no one about the vision until after the Son of Man has been raised from the dead." I still did not understand what he meant about being raised from the dead, but I was not surprised that he told us not to tell anyone. In fact, I did not think I would be able to share this experience with anyone—not then. It was so supernatural, it would have been hard for anyone to believe it even if I could figure out how to explain it. Somehow it seemed best just to let it grow in my heart and soul until the day it was time to let it spring forth and let it be known. Even James and John and I didn't discuss it among ourselves. It was such a mystical experience, we didn't know what to say.

I knew it was a vision—a sign of things to come. "This is my Son, the Beloved; with him I am well pleased; listen to him!" I remember thinking that if I had had anything left to give up for him, I would have done it then. It would be much later when I would realize that I actually had not given up everything for him...yet.

After receiving such a glorious vision of who Jesus was and how I would share in that same glory, I felt willing to go through hell to reach those heavenly heights. Such a vision has the power to change one's life. For now I knew I would do anything for my Lord—the Son of God.

That vision gave us something to hold on to when life would get so very hard. It gave us something to grasp when Jesus had to come down from the mountain and go into the valley that led to the way of the cross.

I believe now that Jesus shared that vision with James, John and me because he wanted us to understand that all that was happening was not just good—it was great—it was amazing! While we could not possibly come close to understanding it, we could certainly appreciate it.

I was finally coming into the realization that the Lord was all-knowing and ever-present in ways I had never known before. He was opening my eyes to things I never before had dreamed I would see. He was giving me a vision to which I could cling.

The Lord wants us all to cling to that vision. He wants us to keep climbing up those spiritual mountains, no matter how steep they may be. Jesus wants us to experience those mountaintop moments that will help us in our difficult days, walking through the valley of life.

God wants to give us all a vision—a vision of the glory that he wants to share with us in our life. This vision is a vision of all we can be. Of course, to do this, we must keep ascending to new heights of holiness to come to that inner vision of who we are and who the Lord is for us.

Jesus invites all of us, just as he invited James, John and me, to come with him in prayer and reflection to receive these insights—to glimpse God's glory.

It is in moments of prayer, reflection and intimate sharing that we come to see our heart's deepest desire, enabling our soul's dreams to be fulfilled in him.

Such moments of grace and glory can truly be a transfiguration—a transformation—of ourselves.

For Reflection

- *Where is your favorite place of prayer and reflection— your mountain—where you can be uplifted, enlightened and inspired?*

- *What is your vision for the future? What do you imagine is God's vision for you?*

- *Can you recall a peak experience in your life that made a deep impression on you? How has this helped in times of difficulty?*

Closing Prayer

"Climb Every Mountain"

Climb every mountain
Ford every stream
Follow every rainbow
'Til you find your dream.
A dream that will need all
   the love you can give
Every day of your life
For as long as you live.

Climb every mountain
Ford every stream
Follow every rainbow
'Til you find your dream.[1]

Notes

1 "Climb Every Mountain," *The Sound of Music,* lyrics by Oscar Hammerstein II, 1965.

DAY FIVE

Serving at the Lord's Table

Coming Together in the Spirit

Reflections by Father Jim

One of the greatest shifts that has occurred in my life since I found out I have cancer has to do with ministry. All of my life as a priest, I have focused on being the minister and, thus, ministering to other people's needs. However, from the day I heard I had cancer, there has been a radical shift that has made me the recipient of others' ministering and caring for me.

And I'll be honest. It was hard for this minister to allow others to minister to him.

It was very humbling and even difficult to accept the fact that I was now in need of people to take care of me. I need to see a number of doctors frequently, and I needed someone to drive me to those frequent visits. I even had to go back to my parents' home on many occasions to recuperate, becoming in every sense, a child again, needing my parents and my brothers and sisters to take care of me.

Once I humbled myself to accept this service, I became aware of an amazing grace that I saw happening in my family. I observed my entire family growing in love as they sacrificed themselves to care for me. I could see them becoming more Christ-like in their loving service.

I, in turn, learned the lesson of the reciprocity of ministry. For it is in giving that we receive, and it is in receiving that we are empowered to give. Only through my family's love and care for me, was I able to carry on my ministry and love and care for others.

This lesson of ministry is hard for us to understand at times. Peter will struggle with this Last Supper lesson, too. But, really, that is the way it has always been. We can only give what we have first received. Jesus wants to teach us all that in order for us to minister and serve others, we must first sit in that humble seat and allow the Lord to pour his love upon us and minister to us.

Opening Prayer

Lord Jesus, cleanse my mind of any thought that is not of you. Lord, have mercy. Christ Jesus, cleanse my heart of any impurity. Christ, have mercy. Lord Jesus, purify my soul of all sins. Lord, have mercy.

Gospel Reading:

Now before the festival of the Passover, Jesus knew that his hour had come to depart from this world and go to the Father. Having loved his own who were in the world, he loved them to the end. The devil had already put it into the heart of Judas son of Simon Iscariot to betray him. And during supper, Jesus, knowing that the Father had given all things into his hands, and that he had come from God and was going to God, got up from the table, took off his outer robe, and tied a towel around himself. Then he poured water into a basin and began to wash the disciples' feet and to wipe them with the towel that was tied around him. He came to Simon Peter, who said to him, "Lord, are you going to wash my feet?"

Jesus answered, "You do not know now what I am doing, but later you will understand." Peter said to him, "You will never wash my feet." Jesus answered, "Unless I wash you, you have no share with me." Simon Peter said to him, "Lord, not my feet only but also my hands and my head!" Jesus said to him, "One who has bathed does not need to wash, except for the feet, but is entirely clean. And you are clean, though not all of you." For he knew who was to betray him; for this reason he said, "Not all of you are clean." After he had washed their feet, had put on his robe, and had returned to the table, he said to them, "Do you know what I have done to you? You call me Teacher and Lord—and you are right, for that is what I am. So if I, your Lord and Teacher, have washed your feet, you also ought to wash one another's feet. For I have set you an example, that you also should do as I have done to you."

...Simon Peter said to him, "Lord, where are you going?" Jesus answered, "Where I am going, you cannot follow me now; but you will follow afterward." Peter said to him, "Lord, why can I not follow you now? I will lay down my life for you." Jesus answered, "Will you lay down your life for me? Very truly, I tell you, before the cock crows, you will have denied me three times." (John 13:1-15, 36-38)

RETREAT SESSION FIVE

It was the night everything changed.

I still cannot believe he did what he did. With one action, Jesus flipped over the hierarchy of class structures we had all come to understand. With one symbolic and prophetic action, he taught us an essential lesson of Christianity.

But, maybe I should start at the beginning. We had all come together for a meal. This, in itself, was not unusual, but from the beginning, I knew that night would be like no other. Perhaps it had to do with the fact that we were finally in Jerusalem. This is where Jesus had told us it all would happen. This is where he would suffer and die. As you can imagine, I was not in a hurry to arrive there.

The reception we received, though, was incredible. Word had spread about Jesus bringing Lazarus back from the dead[1] and many wanted to see Jesus. Multitudes yelled out wonderful things as he rode past them on our way into town. "Hosanna! Blessed is the one who comes in the name of the Lord—the King of Israel!"[2] I was so proud of my Lord. He was finally getting the honor he deserved.

It would only be a few days before all that would change, and it began with the last supper we shared together. We had just settled down for dinner when Jesus stood up from the head of the table. I watched him take off his outer robe and begin to tie a towel around his waist.

What was he doing? I could not imagine he was going to do what it looked like he was about to do. But, as he poured water into a basin, he knelt to begin the chore that only the lowest of household slaves were expected to perform. Jesus knelt down to wash his disciples' feet! This was unheard of! This was unthinkable! Our Master and Teacher was lowering himself to wash our feet.

It was not that we were an unclean group, mind you. But our feet were filthy. You have to understand that we wore nothing but sandals to protect our feet. Therefore, by the end of any given day, after traveling the roads that were covered in mud, filth, dirt and animal droppings, our feet also became covered in the same.

For that reason alone, a host would offer visitors a chance to wash their own feet after a journey, or he would have a slave perform this service. In fact, Hebrew slaves were not even required to stoop so low as to wash feet because it was so degrading. No master of any house would ever consider washing anyone's feet. What could my Master possibly be thinking?

As he approached me, and knelt down before me, it just did not seem right. What was wrong with this picture? In a state of disbelief, I asked, "Lord, are you going to wash my feet?"

As if he knew my question before it was even out of my mouth, he answered, "You do not know now what I am doing, but later you will understand." He certainly was right about my lack of understanding.

Once again, I tried to give him advice. "You will never wash my feet." I felt I said this with the utmost of love and respect. I did not like seeing Jesus lowering himself in this way. I did not like the fact that my Lord had just tied a towel around his waist, assuming both the apparel and position of a slave. I had to admit that part of me was resisting this act of humility since I had come to realize that whatever he did, we were expected to follow. And I certainly had not come this far just to wash people's filthy feet.

It took me a long while to cleanse my mind to a new way of thinking. Just as I had resisted Jesus' prediction of his suffering and death, so again, I was resisting this act of humble service. At least this time, he did not call me Satan.

"Unless I wash you, you have no share with me."

This made no sense to me. If I did not allow Jesus to wash my feet, I would have no part of him? Well, if washing my feet would give me a share of my Lord, I had an even better idea. "Lord, not my feet only but also my hands and my head!"

This time, my childlike frankness seemed to amuse

Jesus. He smiled as he assured me, "One who has bathed does not need to wash, except for the feet, but is entirely clean. And you are clean, though not all of you."

I looked around the room. Which one of us was not clean? I had known Jesus long enough to know that he was not just referring to matters of personal hygiene. He was saying one of us was not clean in some other way. It would be later that night when I would realize that he was referring to Judas—the one who would betray him—as not being pure of heart. I would not find much comfort in that though, as later that night, I would not feel very clean myself. Maybe that is why I had blurted out for Jesus to wash all of me. I knew I was not as clean as I wanted to be and needed to be for my Lord.

When I think back at that moment, I realize that Jesus already knew which one of us was not clean. He knew that Judas would betray him later that very night. Still, Jesus washed his feet as well as all of ours that night. Only Jesus' pure heart could enable him to pour out his unconditional love even on those who would betray him.

I watched in bewildered amazement as Jesus finished his humble chore and then put back on his robe and assumed his rightful place at the head of the table. No one said a word as he did this. Finally, he looked at each and every one of us as he spoke. "Do you know what I have done to you? You call me Teacher and Lord—and you are right, for that is what I am. So if I, your Lord and Teacher, have washed your feet, you also ought to wash one another's feet."

After that, I do not think I said much during the whole meal we shared. I remember sitting there so touched by what I had witnessed. Jesus, our great Teacher and Lord, had humbled himself to wash our feet to beautifully show us that that is what discipleship is all about. To be a follower of his, we must humbly and lovingly serve one another. We are all called to put pride aside and become servants. The difficulty, of course, is that in being servants, we lose any sense of control as we surrender our personal desires, putting the needs of others before our own.

My ideas of what my role as a disciple should be had just flipped upside-down. I was starting to enjoy the idea of being a great leader. Now, Jesus was calling me to be a humble servant. This is to be our role and rule in following Jesus.

Much later, I would have the opportunity to put into practice that which Jesus had taught us. For one day, years later, John and I would come across a crippled beggar asking for alms outside of the temple. At first, I wanted nothing to do with him. I tried to avoid his stare—it made me so uncomfortable. Then I remembered what Jesus had taught us with both his words and actions about serving others. So I gave the crippled man all I had to give by saying to him, "I have no silver or gold, but what I have I give you; in the name of Jesus Christ of Nazareth, stand up and walk."[3] As he stood up for the first time in his life, I truly believe for the first time in *my* life, I understood completely the great paradox that the one who performs such a humble service, such as washing another's feet, is cleansed even more than the one who has been washed.

The very night Jesus washed my feet, I could not completely understand. And I realized that that is okay. We do not have to understand everything. We only have to trust in the Lord.

I trusted Jesus when he went on to tell us, during the meal, about sharing his body and blood with us through the bread and the wine that he had blessed and offered to us. While I could not come close to understanding the significance of that meal, it all was starting to make a little more sense.[4] This, too, was his gift of pouring out his life and love to us in the most humble and loving way.

How blessed I am to know and experience such incredible and unconditional love from my Lord! How blessed we all are!

Later that evening, after supper had ended, I asked the Lord where he was going. "Where I am going, you cannot follow me now; but you will follow afterward." Once again, I did not understand what he wanted me to know. But wherever my Lord was going, I was determined to follow. "Lord, why can I not follow you now? I will lay down my life for you."

I meant every word. There is no one I love more than Jesus. And I know there is no one who loves me more than Jesus loves me. I truly believed I would lay down my life for him. So imagine my shock when Jesus answered me, "Will you lay down your life for me? Very truly, I tell you, before the cock crows, you will have denied me three times."

Never in my life would I have imagined what that meant. But Jesus was never wrong. Though I had not a clue what he meant, this was the beginning of the worst night of my life. How odd that it would follow an evening filled with pure cleansing—a night where love was poured out on us all. Ironically, we disciples had never felt we were as close a community as we were that night at that meal. How all that would change within a few hours!

For Reflection

- *Who is the most loving person you know? What lesson can you learn from that person?*

- *How, specifically, is the Lord calling you to serve others? What is the gift you have been given that you need to share?*

- *How do you allow others to offer their love and service to you?*

Closing Prayer

"Prayer of Saint Francis"

Make me a channel of your peace
Where there is hatred, let me bring your love.
Where there is injury, your pardon, Lord.
And where there is doubt, true faith in you.

Oh, Master, that I may never seek
So much to be consoled, as to console
To be understood, as to understand
To be loved, as to love with all my soul.

Make me a channel of your peace.
It is in pardoning, that we are pardoned.
In giving of ourselves that we receive.
And in dying that we're born to eternal life.[5]

Notes

[1] See John 11:43.

[2] See John 12:12-13.

[3] See Acts 3:6.

[4] See Matthew 26:26-28.

[5] Saint Francis of Assisi, "Prayer of St. Francis," Sebastian Temple.

DAY SIX

Reaching the Depths of Sinfulness

Coming Together in the Spirit

Reflections by Father Jim

Once, shortly after I found out I had cancer, I was praying before the altar at church. Believing I was alone in my prayer, I was startled to have someone come up and put an arm around me and join me by starting to pray. What is more, I was flabbergasted at what she prayed. "Lord, we need Father Jim here. I have had a full life. Give me his cancer and take me instead."

I was incredulous!

And for one brief moment, I was tempted to embrace that thought and actually wanted to encourage the Lord by praying, "Hey—if she insists—Lord, hear our prayer!"

Isn't that like most of us? We are confronted daily with decisions we must make. And some must be made in a split second. When that happens, it is hard to always choose that which is best and not simply easiest—to move out of our first human reaction and on to a more God-inspired second response. When faced with decisions in life, we often become all too aware of our faults and sinfulness. We become awakened to our weakness.

That day at the altar, I did manage to hold my tongue

and not blurt out the first very human reaction that came to me. Instead, I prayed that God would not give that generous lady my cancer, but that he might instead give to me the selfless love that prompted her to make such a beautiful offer.

We all have good and bad in us. And we all need to be awakened to our potential for sin as well as our potential for goodness. Peter is about to learn this the hard way. He is about to fall from his heights of holiness where he felt so confident in his faith. When he falls, he will reach a depth of sinfulness that will break his heart.

We are all given a "wake up call" to stay alert to do as the Lord has requested. If we choose to ignore this request and remain spiritually asleep, we will eventually pay the price.

There is no denying that fact.

Opening Prayer

Jesus, awaken in us your Spirit, so that we may always follow you faithfully.

Gospel Reading:

"Simon, Simon, listen! Satan has demanded to sift all of you like wheat, but I have prayed for you that your own faith may not fail; and you, when once you have turned back, strengthen your brothers." And he said to him, "Lord, I am ready to go with you to prison and to death!" Jesus said, "I tell you, Peter, the cock will not crow this day, until you have denied three times that you know me."

...He came out and went, as was his custom, to the Mount of Olives; and the disciples followed him. When he reached the place, he said to them, "Pray that you may not come into the time of trial." Then he withdrew from them about a stone's throw, knelt down, and prayed, "Father, if you are willing, remove this cup from me; yet, not my will but yours be done." Then an angel from heaven appeared to him and gave him strength. In his anguish he prayed more earnestly, and his sweat became like great drops of blood falling down on the ground. When he got up from prayer, he came to the disciples and found them sleeping because of grief, and he said to them, "Why are you sleeping? Get up and pray that you may not come into the time of trial." While he was still speaking, suddenly a crowd came, and the one called Judas, one of the twelve, was leading them. He approached Jesus to kiss him; but Jesus said to him, "Judas, is it with a kiss that you are betraying the Son of Man?" When those who were around him saw what was coming, they asked, "Lord, should we strike with the sword?" Then one of them struck the slave of the high priest and cut off his right ear. But Jesus said, "No more of this!" And he touched his ear and healed him.

    ... Then they seized him and led him away, bringing him into the high priest's house. But Peter was following at a distance. When they had kindled a fire in the middle of the courtyard and sat down together, Peter sat among them. Then a servant-girl, seeing him in the firelight, stared at him and said, "This man also was with him." But he denied it, saying, "Woman, I do not know him." A little later someone else, on seeing him, said, "You also are one of them." But Peter said, "Man, I am not!" Then about an hour later still another kept insisting, "Surely this man also was with him; for he is a Galilean." But Peter said, "Man, I do not know what you are talking about!" At that moment, while he was still speaking, the cock crowed. The Lord turned and looked at Peter. Then Peter remembered the word of the Lord, how he had said to him,

"Before the cock crows today, you will deny me
three times." And he went out and wept bitterly.
(Luke 22:31-34, 39-51, 54-62)

Retreat Session Six

The mere suggestion of it brought tears to my eyes.
How could I ever deny my Lord? I had felt so
confident in my boast, "Lord, I am ready to go with you
to prison and to death!" But he told me that was not true.
He told me that instead of defending him, I would soon
deny him—before the cock crowed.

How could it be possible that before the sun would
rise on another day, I would deny my Lord? I would
rather die than to deny my Lord. But there was no denying
that he was always right. And there was something about
the way he caught my attention. "Simon, Simon, listen!"

It had been such a long time since he had called me
Simon. As a matter of fact, since he told me my name
was Peter, which meant rock, everyone around me had
begun to call me Peter. And so it definitely sounded odd
to me when he addressed me by the name I had before
he entered my life. But before I could ask why he used
my old name, I was stunned by his prophetic words.
"Satan has demanded to sift all of you like wheat, but I
have prayed for you that your own faith may not fail;
and you, when once you have turned back, strengthen
your brothers."

I realize now that I should have asked what he meant.
Only in looking back, can I see that Jesus was offering to
me the most precious gift of his prayer. He had prayed for
me, knowing how Satan was trying so hard to break us
disciples up so that Jesus' ministry would be ended along

with Jesus' life. It touched me so that he had intentionally singled me out. He had prayed specifically for me! In hindsight, I now understand that it was his prayer alone, that saved my life that night. I will forever be grateful for Jesus' prayer that saved my life.

But at the time I did not have that insight. Instead, my vision was clouded by my pride. I simply boasted that I would never let Jesus down in that way. I suppose, I was in denial about my own weakness long before I ever denied my Lord. I had such an inflated view of myself. This was my sin of pride and presumption. And as they say, "Pride goes before the fall." But I never could have imagined how far I would fall.

The night was getting late. Jesus asked James, John, and me to accompany him to the Garden of Gethsemani. This is where Jesus would often go to pray. Again, I felt honored that he had chosen the three of us to stand by him—the same ones who went to the mountain with him on that blessed day of his transfiguration. I would later be incredibly humbled to realize that he chose us to share in his ecstasy as well as his agony.

As we arrived on the slope of the Mount of Olives, we entered into the garden that had often brought us such peace. Jesus did not go far from us to pray. He was, in fact, only a stone's throw away—though it felt as if we were quite a distance from where he really was. He had only one request for us. He asked that we stay awake and pray.

I tried. I really tried. But it had been an incredibly long day. There was so much to think about. And there was something about that garden that made me feel peaceful and relaxed. What is more, we had all just had a big meal and we had had a little wine. We did what came very naturally.

We all fell fast asleep. Jesus woke us up, not once, not

twice, but three times. Each time he seemed more hurt than the last. Each time, we let him down. I didn't realize how much he needed us then. We were truly asleep to his agony. Jesus was suffering such intense emotional pain while we were completely unaware and unawake to his trauma. So much of that night, I spent sleepwalking in my attempt to follow the Lord.

How I wish I could go back in time and be there for him when he needed me. How I wish I could do what he asked of me and give him the precious gift of my presence and my prayer. What I wouldn't give to be able to wipe his sweat, which fell like great drops of blood.

But like my eyes, my mind was shut to the Lord's request of me. If only I had known then that it is prayer that awakens us to what the Lord is asking. Prayer awakens the spirit in us all.

The last time he came to awaken us from our spiritual slumber, his words were followed by the clamor of a crowd coming toward us. I was finally jarred completely awake as I saw lanterns bobbing in the distance, drawing closer and closer to us. A sense of panic came over me. I wanted to run. I wanted Jesus to run. He could have easily slipped out of sight and no one would have known where he was. But, instead, he calmly stood still as if he were expecting this all to happen.

As the crowd approached, at first, I felt relieved to see Judas leading the way. He was one of us. Surely he had not held a grudge about Jesus telling him that he would be the betrayer. But who were those angry people with him?

I watched as Judas kissed Jesus, and I listened as Jesus responded, "Judas, is it with a kiss that you are betraying the Son of Man?"

Could this be true?! Was Judas actually betraying Jesus? How could he do such a horrible thing? I was outraged! I saw them coming toward my Lord and I instinctively did the only thing I thought I could do. I grabbed my sword and struck at one of the men who had come to take my Lord. I had told Jesus I would defend him, and as long as I had the power to do so, I would. My sword completely took off the ear of the man I struck. But Jesus said, "No more of this!" And he touched the man's ear and healed him.

It never ceases to amaze me that Jesus chose to heal the man who came to hurt him. I marvel at the valor even in his vulnerability. As for me, I realized I had no power whatsoever. Suddenly everything was out of my control.

They seized my Lord and began to take him away. I so badly wanted to go with him—to be by his side. But I couldn't. I was weaker than I ever knew.

In all this confusion, I didn't know where James and John went. For that matter, I didn't know where any of the disciples could be now. All I knew was that in one moment's time, I felt so alone and so afraid. I was not sure which was greater—my Lord's heroic courage, or my own horrific cowardice. I followed my Lord, but only at a distance—a very safe distance. I wonder if that's how I had been following him all along?

It pierced my heart and soul to see the soldiers pushing him around like a common criminal out of the garden and down the Mount of Olives. They led him across the Kidron Valley and up to the house of Caiaphas, the high priest. I could not leave him out of my sight until they led my Lord inside to interrogate him. My fear would not allow me to go any further.

The night was getting colder. Some of the servants of the high priest started a fire in the courtyard to stay warm. I went over to the fire, seeking whatever warmth I could find. I was hoping I could just blend in with the crowd until I heard some news.

A servant girl kept looking at me strangely until she finally said, "This man also was with him." That statement shot panic through my cold heart. Without giving it a second thought the words flew out of my mouth in my own defense, "Woman, I do not know him."

I did not like having to say that, but what else could I do? I was frozen with fright. How I wish I still had my sword—I was so brave with my sword. But Jesus had told me to put it down, and now I was defenseless. I was defenseless and all alone. At least I was still sticking close by, waiting for some word about my Lord. I could have run away like everybody else.

There was still no word yet. The fire kept burning. But it did not warm me. Soon another servant started looking at me in the firelight. "You also are one of them." Again, in my defense, I found myself spewing forth the words, "Man, I am not!" Even I could not believe these words that were falling from my mouth. I had always been so proud to say I was one of his disciples.

About one hour later, the fire was starting to die. But there must have been enough light coming from it, for them to still see my face. "Surely this man also was with him; for he is a Galilean."

Not only had I lost my courage, but I had also lost my faith. I defensively shouted back, "Man, I do not know what you are talking about!"

No sooner had my weak words escaped my mouth than the cock crowed. The night was done. And no sooner had the cock crowed than Jesus, bound like a criminal, was brought out of the house.

I knew he knew. I had denied him three times, just as he had predicted. My friend, my teacher, my Lord—I had shouted to the world that I did not know him—that he meant nothing to me.

Somehow, in spite of the crowd, in spite of what he

was going through, he found me.

His eyes met mine for one incredible and intense moment. And at that very moment, it was excruciating for me to look into the loving and forgiving eyes of Jesus, knowing I had just denied even knowing him. Just as he had predicted, I had denied him. Truthfully, I had betrayed him. I was no better than Judas. I had denied and betrayed my Lord.

I would have understood if he had been furious with me. I would have understood if he had yelled, "I told you so!" across the courtyard. But what he did, instead, I couldn't understand: He continued to love me. For, Jesus looked at me with as much love and compassion as he had ever looked at me before. His eyes clearly communicated across the crowded courtyard his complete forgiveness. And his unconditional and unrelenting love broke my heart.

One of the guards violently pushed my Lord, forcing him to continue. Then he was gone. But his words stayed with me and reverberated in my brain, "Before the cock crows today, you will deny me three times."

That's when I ran away. I did not know where I was running to, but I knew what I was running from. The tears in my eyes made it impossible to see. Because of this, I fell many times. Several times, when I fell I would stay prostrate on the ground, trying to control my sobbing long enough to stand back up again.

I could not stop crying. I would cry for days. I cried my heart out.

I had betrayed my Lord. And when I heard a short while later that Judas had hung himself out of grief, I understood. Later I would come to realize that it was only by the grace of Jesus' earlier prayer for me, that I was kept from taking my own life. At that moment, I could not see ever living with this guilt. Then I heard they were going to crucify him. I couldn't believe this was happening. I had to see for myself.

Making my way through the crowds to Golgotha, the Place of the Skull, I once again, maintained a safe distance. I first caught sight of his mother, Mary. If I thought my pain was unbearable, I cannot imagine what she was feeling. She was clutching her heart as she sobbed at the foot of a cross. Then I looked at that cross. There he was. My Lord was nailed to a tree. One glimpse was all I could take before a violent rush of nausea came over me. I ran away again, sobbing like never before.

I cried because I was not the man I thought I was— the man my Lord needed me to be. I cried because I had denied my Lord. I cried because they were crucifying my Lord.

How I wished I could simply sleep through this nightmare! But nothing about me was asleep anymore. Looking back, this moment of agonizing awakening changed my life in a way that would lead to my greatest conversion and transformation. My life would never be the same again.

True to Jesus' prophetic words of that night, once I turned back, I went to strengthen my brothers. But still, even now, the memory of that night brings tears to my eyes.

For Reflection

- *In what way might you be spiritually sleepwalking— unaware of our Lord's presence?*

- *Have you ever denied the Lord or been untrue to yourself, your faith or a friend?*

- *Can you recall a moment of awakening in your life,*

*through prayer or personal experience, that had a
transforming effect on you?*

Closing Prayer

"Were You There?"

Were you there when they crucified my Lord?
Were you there when they crucified my Lord?
Oh, sometimes it causes me to tremble, tremble,
    tremble.
Were you there when they crucified my Lord?

Were you there when they nailed him to a tree?
Were you there when they nailed him to a tree?
Oh, sometimes it causes me to tremble, tremble,
    tremble.
Were you there when they nailed him to a tree?

Were you there when they laid him in the tomb?
Were you there when they laid him in the tomb?
Oh, sometimes it causes me to tremble, tremble,
    tremble.
Were you there when they laid him in the tomb?[1]

Notes

[1] "Were You There?," African American spiritual.

DAY SEVEN
Receiving Recovery and Reconciliation

Coming Together in the Spirit

Reflections by Father Jim

I have been privileged to make several pilgrimages to Israel. It is always so wonderful to walk in the footsteps of Jesus. Most every sacred site, however, has been affected by change over the years—beautiful basilicas and enchanting cathedrals now stand where once there were none. But the one place in the Holy Land that remains virtually unchanged since the time when Jesus walked the earth is the Sea of Galilee.

On one of these pilgrimages several years ago, I walked along this sacred seashore where Jesus called his first disciples to come and follow him. Upon seeing a fishing boat, I remember being moved to pray, "Lord, I wish I had been one of the fishermen you called. I would have dropped everything to be one of your disciples if you had called me."

And then in that whisper of a voice we can hear from our heart, I heard the Lord respond to me, "Jim, I have called you. Come and follow me."

Since that day, I have been inspired to give my life entirely to the Lord. But, of course, that's a lot easier said than done. It is a daily challenge to surrender my life and my will to the Lord.

Incredibly, it is this cross of cancer that has led me to the greatest surrender of my life and my will to the Lord. I realize that, like Saint Peter, I have had a belt tied around my waist and been led to a place I never would have gone. But it is here that I am being given the opportunity to truly lay down my life and glorify God.

I have no idea what lies ahead, but I can honestly say now that I want to go wherever the Lord leads me. I want to completely give my life to the Lord. I want to be his disciple. Wherever he leads, I will follow.

This also was Peter's wish. He truly wanted to follow the Lord. At the Last Supper, Peter truly wanted to sacrifice his life for the Lord. But he was still relying on his own strength and was unaware of his own weakness. Ironically, it will turn out to be Peter's failure to follow Jesus that will ultimately make him a greater follower and leader. He will come to understand what Jesus meant when he predicted, "I have prayed for you that your own faith may not fail; and you, when once you turn back, strengthen your brothers."[1]

Like Peter, we may deeply desire to surrender our life to the Lord, but this is much easier said than done. As we become painfully aware of our personal sins, weaknesses, and failures, we must allow the Lord to turn us around before we can hope that the Lord will be able to use us to help our own brothers and sisters.

Opening Prayer

Lord, we love you. We love you. We love you. And may our love for you express itself in our love and service to others as well as our openness and willingness to go where you lead, and do whatever you ask.

Gospel Reading:

After these things Jesus showed himself again to the disciples by the Sea of Tiberias; and he showed himself in this way. Gathered there together were Simon Peter, Thomas called the Twin, Nathanael of Cana in Galilee, the sons of Zebedee, and two others of his disciples. Simon Peter said to them, "I am going fishing." They said to him, "We will go with you." They went out and got into the boat, but that night they caught nothing. Just after daybreak, Jesus stood on the beach; but the disciples did not know that it was Jesus. Jesus said to them, "Children, you have no fish, have you?" They answered him, "No." He said to them, "Cast the net to the right side of the boat, and you will find some." So they cast it, and now they were not able to haul it in because there were so many fish. That disciple whom Jesus loved said to Peter, "It is the Lord!" When Simon Peter heard that it was the Lord, he put on some clothes, for he was naked, and jumped into the sea. But the other disciples came in the boat, dragging the net full of fish, for they were not far from the land, only about a hundred yards off. When they had gone ashore, they saw a charcoal fire there, with fish on it, and bread. Jesus said to them, "Bring some of the fish that you have just caught." So Simon Peter went aboard and hauled the net ashore, full of large fish, a hundred fifty-three of them; and though there were so many, the net was not torn. Jesus said to them, "Come and have breakfast." Now none of the disciples dared to ask him, "Who are you?" because they knew it was the Lord. Jesus came and took the bread and gave it to them, and did the same with the fish. This was now the third time that Jesus appeared to the disciples after he was raised from the dead.

When they had finished breakfast, Jesus said to

Simon Peter, "Simon son of John, do you love me
more than these?" He said to him, "Yes, Lord; you
know that I love you." Jesus said to him, "Feed my
lambs." A second time he said to him, "Simon son
of John, do you love me?" He said to him, "Yes,
Lord; you know that I love you." Jesus said to him,
"Tend my sheep." He said to him the third time,
"Simon son of John, do you love me?" Peter felt
hurt because he said to him the third time, "Do you
love me?" And he said to him, "Lord, you know
everything; you know that I love you." Jesus said
to him, "Feed my sheep. Very truly, I tell you, when
you were younger, you used to fasten your own belt
and to go wherever you wished. But when you grow
old, you will stretch out your hands, and someone
else will fasten a belt around you and take you where
you do not wish to go." (He said this to indicate the
kind of death by which he would glorify God.) After
this he said to him, "Follow me." Peter turned and
saw the disciple whom Jesus loved following them;
he was the one who had reclined next to Jesus at the
supper and had said, "Lord, who is it that is going
to betray you?" When Peter saw him, he said to
Jesus, "Lord, what about him?" Jesus said to him, "If
it is my will that he remain until I come, what is that
to you? Follow me!" (John 21:1-22)

Retreat Session Seven

My Lord. My Lord.

On the days that followed his crucifixion, I did not
feel worthy enough to even call his name. I could not
have felt more guilt if I had been the one to pierce his
flesh with the nails.

I had heard that some of the others had taken down

his tortured body and wrapped it with the spices in linen cloths, according to the Jewish burial custom.[2] I knew where the tomb was, but I could not bring myself to go there. I was in too dark a tomb myself.

My darkness was my sinfulness. I could not believe that I had actually denied my Master—my Lord. For so long, I had been "Following the Leader" fairly well, but only until my Leader was out of sight. Then I crumbled. And so, too, had my world. I don't know how we carried on.

On the first day of the following week, Mary Magdalene came running up to John and me. She was in tears. Then again, we all were. But her tears had an urgency about them, "They have taken the Lord out of the tomb and we do not know where they have laid him,"[3] she cried.

I was enraged. What was going on now? Hadn't he suffered enough? John and I took off running to the tomb. John arrived first, but waited for me to arrive before entering. Indeed, the tomb was empty. All that remained were the linen cloths his body had been wrapped in. I picked up one of the cloths and held it to my chest, shaking my head.

John's reaction was different. He walked into the tomb, looked around and nodded his head as if he understood. Without saying a word, we went back home.

Later that day Mary tried to tell us that she had actually seen Jesus again. I could not believe her. I just felt sorry for her.

Then it happened. That night we were meeting in the upstairs room. We had locked the door out of fear. As long as we were in Jerusalem, we did not feel safe. I heard an audible gasp echoing throughout the room. As I looked up, I saw him. It was my Lord. He had walked into the room without ever opening the locked door.

My mouth dropped to my chest as my heart leapt for joy. Then the tears came to me again. My Lord was so close to me. And yet I felt so far from him.

"Peace be with you,"[4] he lovingly said as he breathed the Holy Spirit upon us. I was frozen to my chair. I so badly wanted to go to him, but by the time I found my strength to stand on my own, he was gone. This very scene would be repeated one week later. Again, I wanted to touch him, talk to him, be with him, but I did not get the chance.

So often Jesus would tell us about his suffering, death and resurrection, but I never understood it then and I did not understand it at that moment either. I was so confused. I had mixed feelings of devastation and exaltation. My Lord was no longer a part of this world, but somehow he had come back. I did not know what I was supposed to do. I wished he had told us. Everything we stood for as disciples seemed pointless now that he was gone. Or was he really gone?

After a while I did the only thing that I knew to do. I went back home to Galilee to resume my former way of life. With the death of Jesus, it seemed to me that our discipleship was over. What is more, after my terrible denial of Jesus, I no longer felt worthy to be a disciple. I had no idea what to do—except to start all over again with life as I once knew it—life in Galilee. Everything was simple there. I knew what was going on there. Or so I thought.

Once there, we picked up right where we had left off. I decided to go fishing one night. A few of the other disciples came with me. I was really looking forward to fishing again. I had missed the peacefulness of it all. But somehow it wasn't as rewarding as I had once thought. In fact, it seemed practically pointless. What is more, the night was so dark. But I guess the darkness of the night could not compare with the darkness of my soul.

We had caught absolutely nothing. Jesus was right when he said, "Apart from me you can do nothing."[5] Then a voice came from the shore. The light of the day was just dawning, but I could not see who was calling, "Children, you have no fish, have you?"

How appropriate that we were called children at that time. That is what Jesus would often call us. And that is exactly what we were. We were so very little and what we had mattered so very little. But he was asking about what we didn't have.

We stated the obvious and agreed that we had come up empty all throughout the dark night. The voice from shore continued, "Cast the net to the right side of the boat, and you will find some." Now, why did that sound familiar?

We had nothing to lose. We lowered the nets to the right side of the boat. And it was, indeed, the right side of the boat because within seconds—within seconds—the net was overflowing with fish. It was at that moment that John turned to me and said, "It is the Lord!"

This was the third time I had seen him since I had denied him three times. And this time I was not going to let him get away without talking to him. I had to see him. Without another thought, I jumped into the water and headed toward my Master.

The closer I got to him, the more I realized that I didn't need the dawning of the new day to tell me the Son is risen!

Words cannot express what I felt when Jesus' eyes met mine. It occurred to me that he was absolutely glowing just as he was on the day we were on the Mountain of Transfiguration! He looked more alive than ever before.

There was a charcoal fire burning, and fish and bread already waiting for us. I didn't have to ask where the feast had come from. I already knew.

Because I was soaking wet, I should have been cold and headed straight to the fire, but unlike the last fateful time I stood shivering before a charcoal fire, this time I finally felt warm.

Somehow I knew I would get my chance with him on that day. But first, I had to do my part in helping to bring in the great catch. I have heard that there are 153 kinds of fish in the sea. It dawned on me that we caught one of each kind, yet the net never broke. Could this be Jesus' prophetic way of indicating to us how we were to draw all nations into the Church, and promising us that the Church would not be torn—or divided?

We ate what he had prepared for us. I couldn't help but remember the last supper we shared. And though it now seemed like a lifetime ago, I couldn't help but remember what had happened after that meal. Jesus knew my very thoughts.

He came over to me. While his eyes were as loving as they could be, I was prepared for the worst. What would he say to me? No matter how bad it would be, I would take it. I deserved it. I was ready.

"Simon, son of John, do you love me more than these?"

While I wasn't expecting that question, I knew just where it had come from. Jesus always gets to the heart of the matter. It hadn't been that long ago since I boasted during the Last Supper, "Even though all will become deserters, I will not."[6]

Wherever he was going with this, I deserved it. How proud I had been! How weak I had been! At least the lessons of the last weeks had not been lost on me. This time I had nothing to boast about. I had no empty promises to make. All I could offer was the humble truth. "Yes, Lord; you know that I love you."

And Jesus replied, "Feed my lambs."

Before I had a chance to question him about what that meant, he continued on, "Simon son of John, do you love me?"

Again, he asked me the same question. Again, he called me Simon. Again, I answered him, "Yes, Lord; you know that I love you." This time his response was only slightly different. "Tend my sheep."

And for the third time, my Lord questioned my love. "Simon son of John, do you love me?" Now, I understood that I had no right to expect Jesus to take me at my word. I had given him my word before, only to let him down. I knew that I deserved to never have Jesus' trust again. But still, I have to admit that it hurt my feelings that he had asked me three times. Only later would I realize that it was love, not distrust, that prompted Jesus to ask me to affirm my love for him the same number of times that I had denied him.

At that moment though, I didn't understand, "Lord, you know everything; you know that I love you." With that he simply said, again, "Feed my sheep."

At this time I was looking into his eyes. I realized the others were still around, but somehow they had all faded into the background. It was just my Lord and I having this intimate conversation. I could see such forgiveness and tender mercy in his eyes. There was no longer a shred of doubt that Jesus had completely forgiven me and even loved me all the more. And at that moment, being so unconditionally and intimately loved, I felt for the first time, my mind and my heart opening to the gift of forgiving myself. This process would take much longer to mature and deepen in me, but I'll never forget that moment when his eyes allowed me to see myself in a new way, and his heart allowed me to love and forgive myself in that same way.

And now I so badly wanted to be able to understand

what it was he was asking of me. He needed me to understand. I looked deeper into his eyes. At last, I was truly beginning to comprehend.

Jesus had always been such a wonderful shepherd for us. He knew he needed someone to be the Chief Shepherd when he would have to leave us again. Much like he had given me the keys to the kingdom on the day he changed my name from Simon to Peter, he was now asking me to tend to the needs of his flock—his disciples. I cannot put into words how honored and how humbled I felt. I was stunned! After all I had done—after all I had not done— Jesus was asking me to take on this important position that I didn't deserve in the least. For now, the reality of how I had sinned had become so brutally clear to me. I had failed so terribly as a follower, but somehow, he was asking me to now be a leader.

I wanted to point all this out to him, but I knew that Jesus knew me better than I could ever know myself. How ironic that earlier I had been the one who had tried to tell Jesus to put a limit on the number of times we should forgive one another. I vividly remember Jesus teaching us disciples about forgiveness. I had asked, "...Lord, if another member of the church sins against me, how often should I forgive? As many as seven times?" Thankfully, Jesus answered me, "...Not seven times, but, I tell you, seventy-seven times" (Matthew 18:21-22). At that time I could not possibly understand what a precious gift forgiveness truly is.

Jesus was offering this precious gift to me. What is more, in this forgiveness, my Lord was giving me a chance to not just tell him I love him, but to show him I love him.

I simply nodded my head, still looking into those eyes. There was something about his eyes that reminded me of the way he looked at me during our conversation after our last supper together. This was when he had told me that he had prayed for me that my faith would not fail, and once I turned back, I would strengthen my brothers.[7] A realization washed over me. Was this what it was all about? Again, I felt so humbled by it all.

What Jesus said next would take me a lifetime to figure out. "Very truly, I tell you, when you were younger, you used to fasten your own belt and to go wherever you wished. But when you grow old, you will stretch out your hands, and someone else will fasten a belt around you and take you where you do not wish to go."

I have to admit that old habits die hard. The first thing in my mind flew immediately out of my mouth as I saw John walking toward us. "Lord, what about him?" I childishly asked. Jesus, who had every right to grow exasperated with me, calmly answered, "If it is my will that he remain until I come, what is that to you? Follow me!"

These words should have frightened me. But I was not afraid. It had not been that long since Jesus had told me about his impending suffering and dying. That prediction petrified me. I was not ready to even think about Jesus suffering. I was not ready to think about myself suffering. But after everything that happened, I was learning to listen. And I was hearing Jesus call me to surrender my entire life to him. At that very moment, I knew I was no longer in control of my life.

In my early years, I had always felt in control. I was my own boss. I made the decisions. I did not realize then what an illusion I had been living. We think we are in control of our lives. But the reality is, so much of what we think we're handling, is completely out of our grasp. It is only when we turn our life over to the Lord that he turns our life into what it was meant to be. It wasn't until I gave up everything to follow the Lord that I realized how full my life could be.

I realized then that I would not be returning to my former way of life. I would spend the rest of my life as a fisher of people. My life was completely committed to the Lord now.

Thirty years later, in Rome, I would be given the opportunity to stretch out my arms and truly lay down my life for the Lord. And what a gift it was to lay down my life for the one who laid down his life for me!

That morning beside the fire, in Galilee, turned out to be my last visit and conversation with the Lord. For that reason the words he spoke to me are all the more precious. And I will never forget that his last words to me were also his very first words to me, "Follow me." My Lord called me twice at the very same spot by the sea. He looked at me and simply said, "Follow me."

And I did.

We have all failed and sinned in one way or another— none of us has been perfect. We are all weak. But all that matters to the Lord is the answer to his question that he will ask us all one day, "Do you love me?"

It's not enough to simply *tell* him we love him. We must *show* him. And we show him by loving and serving others. It is through that love and service that we are given the opportunity to truly follow him.

Being a disciple is not easy. It is, indeed, full of challenges and hardships. But it is also full of joy and wonder. I would not have traded it for the world—even the part about losing my life.

Because, you see, being a disciple can honestly cost you your life. But in return, you will be given eternal life.

For Reflection

- *How are you being called to surrender your life more completely to the Lord and sacrifice yourself for others?*

- *How are you being called to show your love and commitment to the Lord through love and service to others?*

- *Have you ever had trouble forgiving yourself? Have you ever experienced one of your worst failures turning into one of your best lessons?*

Closing Prayer

"Just a Closer Walk with Thee"

Just a closer walk with thee
Grant it, Jesus, is my plea
Daily walking close to thee.
Let it be, dear Lord, let it be.
I am weak but thou art strong
Jesus, keep me from all wrong
I'll be satisfied as long
As I walk, let me walk close
    to thee.
Through this world of toll and
    snares
If I falter, Lord, who cares?
Who, with me, my burden shares?
None but thee, dear Lord, none
    but thee.
When my feeble life is o'er
Time for me will be no more
Guide me gently, safely o'er
To thy kingdom shore, to thy shore.

Just a closer walk with thee
Grant it, Jesus, is my plea
Daily walking close to thee
Let it be, dear Lord, let it be.[8]

Notes

1. Luke 22:31.
2. John 19:40.
3. John 20:13.
4. John 20:19.
5. John 15:5.
6. Matthew 26:33.
7. Luke 22:31.
8. "Just a Closer Walk with Thee."

Going Forth to Live the Theme

Where do I end?

To tell the truth, the journey of following the Lord never really ends. It is a continuous process.

The journey is never easy. For when we answer the call of the Lord, we must surrender our lives and our will to him. And that, too, is a continuous process. When I finally stopped playing Simon Says and began to Follow the Leader my empty nets and my emptiness were filled beyond belief. But that doesn't mean I had learned enough at that point. Heaven knows I had a long way to go.

Every day we are called to walk on water, by walking in faith. Many of these times we start off with the best of intentions—we step out in great faith. But soon we find ourselves drowning in doubts, falling into fear, sinking into sadness. This is the time we must realize that if we have truly surrendered our lives to the Lord, we know we only have to call out to him for help and his loving hand will save us.

That same loving hand keeps leading us further on this journey of faith. Jesus will constantly keep encouraging us to keep growing in our understanding of who he is and who we are in our relationship to him. There will be times when we will feel truly inspired by the Lord. We will feel as solid as a rock. Still, other times, we will be fighting the devil himself as we realize we have, indeed, become a stumbling block.

On those good days, we can sense this ascent to a new height of holiness. These are the times when we will feel blessed with a spiritual experience and insight that makes us feel as if we are on a mountaintop, catching a glimpse of what is to come. Though it would only be natural for us to want to stay there, we will realize we must take those experiences and visions with us and return to the valley and to the journey that challenges each one of us in life.

Along this spiritual journey, there will be many opportunities to serve one another at the Lord's table. Because it is only in the humble service of one another that we can truly imitate our Lord—who poured out his love for others.

But no matter how good our intentions may be, we will often find that we painfully fail the Lord. We find ourselves falling into the depths of sinfulness, not knowing how to get out of such a black hole. And the truth is, we cannot save ourselves. It is purely Jesus' mercy that saves us from our misery.

All that really matters to the Lord, though, is that we love him, love him, love him, and that we express this love—show love—through our genuine love and service of one another. It is this love that will always heal us and restore us to a right relationship with God and others, allowing us to receive recovery and reconciliation.

No, the journey is not an easy one. But it is an amazing one.

And no matter where you are on this journey of faith, always remember you are not alone. Jesus is walking beside you just as he walked beside me. Just like many years ago when he first came to me, he is now coming to you, inviting you to grow from sinner to saint.

And it all begins right here, right now, as Jesus says to you, "Follow me."

Deepening Your Acquaintance

Books

Grant, Michael. *Saint Peter: A Biography*, Michael Grant
Publications, Ltd., 1994.

Ray, Stephen K. *Upon This Rock: St. Peter and the Primacy of
Rome in Scripture and the Early Church*, Modern
Apologetics Library.

Brown, Raymond E., S.S., Joseph A. Fitzmeyer, S.J., and
Roland E. Murphy, O. Carm. *The New Jerome Biblical
Commentary*, Prentice Hall, Inc., New Jersey, 1990.

Brown, Raymond, Karl P. Donfried, and John Reumann.
Peter in the New Testament, Paulist Press, New York,
1973.

Willig, Jim, and Tammy Bundy. *Lessons from the School of
Suffering: A Young Priest With Cancer Teaches Us How to
Live*, St. Anthony Messenger Press, Cincinnati, 2001.

Videos

The Passion and Resurrection of our Lord Jesus Christ,
dramatized by J. Michael Sparough, S.J., with reflections
by Rev. Jim Willig. Available from "Heart to Heart."